Evolution and Development of Islamic Jurisprudence in Central Asia

Islamic Heritage in Cross-Cultural Perspectives

1. Gandhi's Responses to Islam; by Sheila McDonough. (ISBN 978-81-246-0035-1)
2. Fawā'id al-Fu'ād — Spiritual and Literary Discourses of Shaikh Niẓāmuddīn Awliyā; Originally Compiled by Amīr Ḥasan 'Alā' Sijzī Dehlawī; English Translation with Introduction and Historical Annotation by Ziya-ul-Hasan-Faruqi. (ISBN 978-81-246-0042-9)
3. Change and Continuity in Indian Sūfism — A Naqshbandi-Mujaddidī Branch in the Hindu Environment; Thomas Dahnhardt. (ISBN 978-81-246-0170-9)
4. Islamic Thought and Movement in the Subcontinent — A Study of Sayyid Abu A'lā Mawdudi and Sayyid Abul Hasan Ali Nadwi; Sheikh Jameil Ali. (ISBN 978-81-246-0491-5)
5. Ṣūfī Thought of Shaikh Sayyid 'Abdul Qādir Jīlānī and Its Impact on the Indian Subcontinent; Manzoor Ahmad Bhat. (ISBN 978-81-246-0545-5)
6. Islamic Resurgence: Sayyid Abul Ḥasan 'Ali Nadwī and his Contemporaries; Abdul Kader Choughley. (ISBN 978-81-246-0573-8)
7. Sayyid Abul Ḥasan 'Ali Nadwī: Life and Works; Abdul Kader Choughley. (ISBN 978-81-246-0611-7)

Islamic Heritage in Cross-Cultural Perspectives, no. 8

Evolution and Development of Islamic Jurisprudence in Central Asia (CE 750–1258)

Dr Showkat Hussain Dar

DK PRINTWORLD
Publishers of Indian Traditions

Cataloging in Publication Data — DK
[Courtesy: D.K. Agencies (P) Ltd. <docinfo@dkagencies.com>]

Dar, Showkat Hussain, 1975-
Evolution and development of Islamic jurisprudence in Central Asia (CE 750-1258) / Showkat Hussain Dar.
p. cm. – (Islamic heritage in cross-cultural perspectives ; no. 8)
Includes bibliographical references (p.).
ISBN 13: 9788124607237

1. Islamic law – Asia, Central. I. Title. II. Series: Islamic heritage in cross-cultural perspectives ; no. 8.

DDC 340.590958 23

First published in India, 2014
ISBN 13: 978-81-246-0723-7

Published and printed by:
D.K. Printworld (P) Ltd.
Regd. Office: 'Vedaśrī', F-395, Sudarshan Park
(Metro Station: Ramesh Nagar)
New Delhi – 110 015
Phones: (011) 2545 3975; 2546 6019; *Fax*: (011) 2546 5926
e-mail: indology@dkprintworld.com
Website: www.dkprintworld.com

Preface

THE vast territory of Central Asia has remained among the heartlands of Islam since second/eighth century CE. The region, in the chronicles of the Islamic history, has been identified and referred by the name Mawara al-Nahr (Transoxiania), the territory beyond the river Jayhun (Oxus). It was during the reign of the Umayyad caliph Hisham (AH 724-43) that his eminent governor, Qutaybah bin Muslim conquered this vast territory and annexed it with the Islamic caliphate from CE 712-15. The Umayyad reign (CE 661–750), after introducing Islam, could not go beyond the construction of the mosques and rehabilitating the Muslims in this region. However, these efforts paved the way for setting the Islamic culture as well as the Muslim identity in this region. Henceforth, Muslim institutions, be it social or political got momentum to maintain identity in the steppe. With the establishment of the Abbasid rule (CE 750–1258), positive results and impact of the Islamic ideology could be seen in almost all aspects of the community life. The socio-intellectual activities of the Muslims proved to be much constructive to cultivate the high academic and institutional set-up in this region. Since then, it has evolved as an illustrious region that nourished the Islamic tradition and made renowned contribution to the various socio-political institutions as well as diverse fields of knowledge. Central Asia, being located at a pivotal position both geographically as well as culturally, influenced the entire landmass and set a consummate landmark in developing Islamic sciences in a systematic manner. The early development of the Islamic sciences and involvement of the Muslim intellectuals of Central Asia will always remain as a splendid chapter of the Islamic history.

The present work, *Evolution and Development of Islamic Jurisprudence in Central Asia*, represents Islam1 as a constructive force that nourished a versatile scholarship into a variety of Islamic sciences (*'ulum*) especially in the field of Islamic jurisprudence. The Islamic legal theory and its development in various phases encompass various regions, intellectual approaches and social practices that broadened its horizon to mature as an appropriate legal system. Along the Muslim intellectual centres like Baghdad, Basrah, Kufa and Medina, the cities of Central Asia maintained the lure of standardized scholarship as analysed in the proceeding chapters of the present work.

The first chapter, "Introduction" is the conceptual background of the evolution and development of the Islamic legal theory in Central Asia. The chapter, simultaneously, narrates the process of the expansion of Islam beyond Arabia and approaches of the Muslim jurists regarding interpretation and application of the legal theory. This chapter also examines the development of various branches of learning and concern of the ruling dynasties for the cultivation of the academic endeavour. The second chapter, "Review of the Source Material" discusses and elaborates the source material pertaining to the study of Islamic jurisprudence as well as its introduction in Central Asia. This particular constituent endorses the relevant material of Islamic jurisprudence compiled in different languages throughout the Islamic lands. The third chapter, "Socio-Political Milieu" elaborates and discusses socio-political milieu of Central Asia from CE 750–1258 in addition to the concentration upon the intellectual activities especially during the period under consideration. This chapter also acknowledges the efforts of various ruling dynasties and scholars that took pride in patronizing the knowledge tradition and transmitting it to the forthcoming generations. The chapter, as such, envisions the establishment of an absolute academic endeavour that proved to be a distinction to the Islamic legacy. The forth chapter, "Central Asian Jurists: Contribution and Impact" is a detailed account of the reputed jurists who contributed an immense share to the development of Islamic jurisprudence. This chapter is exclusively dedicated to analyse the legal dynamism of the Muslim jurists who formed the basis for the study and interpretation of legal discourse by virtue of compiling monumental works in this field. Their concentration upon the primary sources of the law (Quran and Sunnah) and interpretation of a commandment (*hukm al-shara'i*) to go well with the circumstances will also be studied. The fifth chapter, "Prolific Centres of Islamic Jurisprudence" recognizes the major centres of Muslin intellectualism in Central Asia that played a significant role for the promotion and dissemination of the Islamic sciences. The last chapter "Conclusion", sums up the whole narrative and initiates a debate regarding relevance of the Islamic legal theory and its interpretation in the contemporary socio-political scenario. The debate is relevant as it explores certain possibilities of rediscovering Islamic jurisprudence for the present times.

9 November 2013 **Dr Showkat Hussain Dar**

Contents

Acknowledgement

IT really gives me an immense pleasure to express a deep sense of gratitude to a number of persons and institutions for the support and inspiration while working on this book. At the very outset, I feel privileged to acknowledge all my teachers who infused in me the love for knowledge as well as the spirit of investigation and research aptitude. Prof. G.N. Khaki, Centre of Central Asian Studies (CCAS), University of Kashmir, in whom I have found an affectionate teacher deserves special and sincere recognition. I am also thankful to the teachers of S.H. Institute of Islamic Studies, University of Kashmir, for their considerable support and encouragement. I am highly grateful to the Library Staff of Dar al-'Ulum Sopore, Dar al-'Ulum Raheemia, Bandipora; Khuda Bakhsh Oriental Library, Patna (Bihar); Library CCAS, University of Kashmir; Allama Iqbal Library; The University of Kashmir; Raza Library, Rampur (UP); Dar al-'Ulum Nadwah al-'Ulama, Lucknow (UP); and Dar al-'Ulum Deoband (UP) for providing access to the useful material during execution of this work.

I am indebted to the institutional support of Islamic University of Science and Technology, Awantipora, J&K, an encouragement and solace that will grow everlasting. I am also indebted to my colleagues and friends in the Islamic University of Science and Technology who had been so cordial and amiable.

I am highly indebted to acknowledge and thank my parents, wife Jameela Akhtar, brother M. Rafiq and children

Faheem and Tassaduq for the extensive support and encouragement throughout the preparation of this work. Last but not the least special thanks to D.K. Printworld, New Delhi for publishing this work with extensive care.

Transliteration

In this book, I have adopted the most recent rules of transliteration recognized by the reputed Muslim and Western scholars of Islamic studies with very slight variation, as explained in the table. Nevertheless, no transliteration can exactly express the vocalic differences of two languages, and the Roman characters in which Arabic words and phrases have been spelt give the sound of the original only approximately. Besides the inability of the characters of one language to represent the exact pronunciation of the words of another, there is this additional difficulty in Romanizing Arabic words that in certain combinations the pronunciation does not follow the written characters; for example, *al-Rahim* is pronounced *ar-Rahim*, the sound of *l* merging in that of the next following letter, *r*. To this category belong all the letters which are known by the name of *al-Huruf al-Shamsiyyah*. Whenever a word beginning with one of these letters has the prefix *al* (representing the article *the*), the *lam* is passed over in pronunciation and assimilated to the following consonant; in the case of all other letters, *al* is pronounced fully. This merging of one letter in another occurs also in certain other cases, for which a grammar of the Arabic language should be referred to. The system adopted is as follows:

Consonants

Arabic Letter	*Sounds*	*Represented by*
hamzah	Sounds like *h* in *hour* — a sort of catch in the voice	'
ba	Same as *b*	*b*
ta	The Italian dental, softer than *t*	*t*
tha	Between *th* in *thing* and *s*	*th*
jim	Like *g* in *gem*	*j*
fa	Very sharp but smooth guttural aspirate	*f*
kha	Like *ch* in the Scotch word *loch*	*kh*
dal	Italian dental, softer than *d*	*d*
dhal	Sounds between *z* and *th* in *that*	*dh*
ra	Same as *r*	*r*
za	Same as *z*	*z*
sin	Same as *s*	*s*
shin	Same as *sh* in *she*	*sh*
sad	Strongly articulated *s*, like *ss* in *hiss*	*s*
zad	Aspirated *d*, between *d* and *z*	*dz*
ta	Strongly articulated palatal *t*	*t*
za	Strongly articulated palatal *z*	*z*
'ain	Somewhat like a strong guttural *hamzah*, not a mere vowel	'
ghain	Gutteral *g*, but soft	*gh*
fa	Same as *f*	*f*
qaf	Strongly articulated guttural *k*	*q*
kaf	Same as *k*	*k*
lam	Same as *l*	*l*

Consonants (Contd.)

Arabic Letter	*Sounds*	*Represented by*
mim	Same as *m*	*m*
nun	Same as *n*	*n*
ha	Same as *h*	*h*
waw	Same as *w*	*w*
ya	Same as *y*	*y*

Vowels

The vowels (*Huruf al-'illah*) are represented as follows:

Short vowels	
'fatfah, as *u* in tub	*a*
'kasrah, as *i* in pin	*i*
Long vowels	
Long fatfah, as *a* in father	*a*
Long kasrah, as *ee* in deep	*i*
Long ammah, as *oo* in moot	*u*
fatfah before *waw*	*au*
fatfah before *ya*	*ai*
Tanwin " " "	*an, in, un,* respectively

1

Introduction

'Ilm al-Fiqh (the science of Islamic jurisprudence) is one of the core disciplines of Islamic studies. As a special branch of the Islamic knowledge system, it has developed through various phases, and the history of its development simultaneously runs along with the history of Islamic civilization.[1] The Arabic word *fiqh* is a derivation from *tafaquh* which literally means the absolute understanding. The term has also been used to denote the *appropriate understanding* to know the essence of the commandments (*ahkam*) prescribed in Quran and Sunnah.[2] Technically, the term *fiqh* refers to the knowledge of deducing laws and verdicts from the basic sources of Shari'ah namely Quran and Sunnah.[3] Thus the science of Islamic jurisprudence treats Quran and Sunnah as the origin and the primary source of Shari'ah. The primary sources mentioned here constitute the foundation as well as the core of Shari'ah.

The Quran was revealed in peacemeal fashion in fragments and sections required as per the circumstances to facilitate the understanding of the text, value its relevance and implant gradually its norms for the final implementation. The revealed book has been preserved, word for word, in its complete and original form to serve as a source of guidance for all the times

---

1 Ahmad bin Muhammad, *Usul al-Shashi*, Beirut, 1982, pp. 9-10.

2 Quran, 9:123.

3 Ahmad bin Muhammad, op. cit., p. 10.

and situations. Quran provides a general theoretical framework containing universal and practical rules, principles, exhortations and commandments which are manifest, sublime and blessed. The Quranic verses have been classified into three categories as per the plan of instruction; the articles of faith, the ethical and legal instructions, and the regulations concerning state and society. The bulk of the Quranic content is ethical and moral. The legal prescriptions deal as per the situation enabling society to identify itself as per the Quranic reflection. The Sunnah consists of all the authentic reports of the acts, utterances and tacit approval of the Prophet Muhammad (SAW). Initially, there existed a distinction between the terms Sunnah referring to the practices of the prophet and *Hadith* denoting his utterances as narrated by his companions. Gradually, with the passage of time, however, the entire Sunnah was reflected in *Hadith* to such an extent that by the fifth century AH, the two terms became completely synonymous. Quran is definitive as well as final and authoritative as a whole and in its detail. Sunnah is neither definitive nor final or authoritative in its detail but must be taken as a whole. There are three possible relations of Sunnah to Quran. The first is where Sunnah agrees with Quran in all respects, and in such a case the two corroborate and reinforce the given point. The second is where Sunnah explains and illustrates Quran and the third is where Sunnah legislates on a matter on which Quran is silent. No other possibilities exist for Sunnah can never run counter to Quran.

The secondary sources of Shari'ah include all those methods and procedures employed by the Muslim jurists to comprehend and operationalize the divine will as contained in Quran and Sunnah. Hence the word *fiqh* (Islamic jurisprudence), during the earlier phase of Islamic era (first century AH), had a comprehensive and vast meaning; to denote besides Quran and its interpretation, the accurate knowledge of the legal decisions passed on by the Prophet (SAW) and his companions to the forthcoming generations.[4] To interpret Quran or Sunnah with a view to deduce legal verdicts (*ahkam al-shara'i*) from the indications (*ishrah al-nass*), the science of jurisprudence emerged as a substantial discipline trying to reveal the best that could suit the circumstances without any contradiction to the basic sources. So it is necessary that the language of Quran and Sunnah be clearly approached and understood. To be able to utilize these sources, *mujtahid* (legal expert) must obtain a firm grasp of the words of the text and their precise as well as broad implications. For this purpose, *'ulama* of *'usul* includes the classification of words and their usages in the methodology of *usul al-fiqh*. The rules that govern the origin of words, their usages and classification are primarily determined on linguistic grounds and, as such, they are not an integral part of the law or religion. However, they are instrumental as an aid to the correct understanding of Shari'ah. Normally *mujtahid* will not resort to interpretation when the text itself is self-evident and clear. However, by far the greater part of *fiqh* consists of rules, which are derived through interpretation and *ijtihad* (exertion). As will be discussed later, *ijtihad* can take a variety of forms, and interpretation, aiming at the correct understanding of words and sentences of a legal text, is of crucial significance to all forms of *ijtihad*. The function of interpretation is to discover the intention of the lawgiver — or of any person for that matter — from his speech and actions. Interpretation is primarily concerned with the discovery of that which is not self-evident. Thus the objective of interpretation in Islamic Law, as in any other law, is to ascertain the intention of the lawgiver with regard to what has been left unexpressed as a matter of necessary inference from the surrounding circumstances. Thus, the legal verdicts

[4] W.B. Hallaq, *A History of Islamic Legal Theories*, Cambridge, 1997, p. 47.

of Quran and Sunnah are to be properly interpreted to make any possibility of further legal discourse. Simultaneously, along the compilation of *Hadith* and *Sirah* literature, the legal precepts were preserved and passed on through the authority of most learned and reliable men to be consulted while resolving and providing the legal references on specific occasions.[5]

The science of Islamic jurisprudence, in its developed form, came to recognize a variety of sources, methods and approaches from and through which laws and rulings may be derived.[6] With the result of this process, different schools of law (*madahib*) within Islam formulated their legal interpretations to unveil the nature and derivatives of the revealed commandments. The primary sources of the Islamic law, Quran and *Hadith* provide the basis and subject matter of the legal theory. While as the secondary sources, through which the law may be derived, represent the methods of *qiyas* (reasoning) or the sanctioning instrument of *ijma* (consensus) and are still identified as the valid sources of the Islamic law.[7] In addition to this, *ijtihad* (exertion), *urf* (custom), *istehsan* (juristic preference), *istidlal* (referring) and *masaliah al-mursalah* (the law of suitability) are among the approved legal tools that have been identified and applied as the alternate methods for the deduction of law.[8] The classical juristic schools of the Islamic jurisprudence interpreted and discussed all these alternate vehicles to support their arguments while conforming the appropriate judgement. As a result, both, *hukm* (precept) and *zaman* (time) acted together and formulated the deducting principles for understanding and resolving the confronting

[5] W.B. Hallaq, *A History of Islamic Legal Theories*, Cambridge, 1997, p. 49.

[6] D.B. Macdonald, *Development of Theology Jurisprudence and Constitutional Theory*, Cambridge, 1903, pp. 43-45.

[7] Ibid., p. 44.

[8] Hallaq, op. cit., p. 165.

issues. This process resulted in the development of the Islamic legal theory and provided *imkan* (chance) for rediscovery of further advance debate in this discipline.

In fact, the development of Islamic jurisprudence can be divided into distinct phases that extended its scope and explored new dimensions to its vast study. This process began during the first century AH/CE 622 with the fresh revelations of Quran in order to promote the concept of socio-economic justice and the unity of God (*Tawhid*). In the primary phase, the legislation took place through *wahy* (Quranic revelations) and the prophetic instructions defined their ultimate application. The second phase extends from the Prophet's demise and ultimately covers the time of *suhabah* (companions) and their *taba'in* (successors). This particular phase of the legal history is crucial and is earmarked with the compilation of *nusus* (legal verdicts), *rai* (opinions), *fatawa* (decrees and decisions) and *ijtihad* of the companions and their successors to deal with the socio-economic and political issues.[9]

The legislation, especially under the first four caliphs (CE 632-60) and *athar al-sahabah* (interpretation of the learned companions of the Prophet), is considered to be the much authentic and reliable source of the Islamic jurisprudence besides Quran and Sunnah. This phase is considerably significant for the exploration of adopted methods in an absolute legislative form. The third phase of the social interaction saw many appropriate and revolutionary trends that also widened the scope of legal discourse in Islam. *Taba'in* and their followers (*taba taba'in*) introduced innovative legal approaches to expand the spectrum of Islamic jurisprudence as a special study. With the extension of the Muslim caliphate (Umayyad era CE 661–750), new ideas and socio-economic challenges confronted the state and the exigent circumstances

[9] Sarakhsi, *al-Usul*, Cairo, 1973, p. 68.

demanded speedy disposal of issues. Muslim intellectuals, at this moment, thought for the alternate methods of deduction to settle the issues in light of the primary sources.[10]

Islamic jurisprudence, as it occurs, has never been a rigid, stagnant or inexplicable concept. It is firmly rooted and established upon the concrete foundations of *wahy* (revelation), *'aql* (reason) and *istensan* (public good). The legal expertise saw an upsurge and exemplary concern with the beginning of second century AH. In this learned venture, both Arabs and non-Arabs (*'ajm*) contributed for developing methodological tools through and by which the science of Islamic jurisprudence came to be recognized within the Islamic sciences.[11] With the process of the expansion of the caliphate and administration of the newly-conquered territories, the legal expertise had to face a variety of challenges. The matters of fiscal, socio-economic nature widened the scope of legal discourse and a dynamic study was carried out to transmit this discipline to the far off regions of the Muslim caliphate. Around AH 160, the science of Islamic jurisprudence entered to a systematic phase as *kutub al-usul* (doctrinal treatises) added splendour to the study of legal philosophy.[12] It was during this period that three renowned geographical divisions Hejaz, Iraq and Syria established centres *par excellence* pertaining various branches of knowledge. Iraq, a predominant centre of learning, had three recognized scholastic seats at Basrah, Baghdad and Kufa.[13]

Hejaz (Arabia), on the other hand, had two great seats of learning at Mecca and Medina. This particular region had tilt towards *zahir* (literal understanding) of the prophetic traditions and had gained conformity and say over the jurists. They,

---

10 N.J. Coulson, *A History of Islamic Law*, Edinburg, 1990, p. 87.

11 Ibid., p. 44.

12 Hallaq, op. cit., p. 52.

13 Ibid., p. 51.

sometimes, as has been reported by the contemporary sources, resisted against the interpretations of the Iraqi jurists who conformed the approved social experiences as valid sources of the law. *Muhadithin* (traditionists) hardly borrowed any ruling from elsewhere and remained strict adherents of Quran and *Ahadith*.[14] Syria, as the caliphate seat of the Umayyads (CE 661–750) had a centre of jurisprudence at Damascus where the process of legislation produced towering figures of the high intellect.[15] The Iraqi School of Islamic jurisprudence is ascribed to Hazrat 'Ali (d. CE 661), 'Abdullah bin Mas'ud (d. CE 671) and their disciples. The further extension of this school was lead by 'Alqamah (d. AH 62), Shuraih bin Harith (d. AH 78), Aswad bin Yazid (d. AH 75), Masruq (d. AH 63), Ibrahim Nakha'i (d. AH 96), Sh'abi (d. AH 103), Hammad bin Salma (d. AH 120), Abu Hanifa (d. AH 150) and his reputed disciples Abu Yusuf (d. AH 182), Muhammad bin Hasan al-Shaybani (d. AH 189) and Zufr (d. AH 192).[16] As a result, the Iraqi School transmitted authentic and reliable interpretations to triumph over the exigent socio-political circumstances.

As the boundaries of the Muslim caliphate extended towards Mawara al-Nahr (Transoxiania/Central Asia), Sindh (Indus) and Andalus (Spain), a variety of socio-economic and political issues widened the scope of legal discourse.[17] However it was not the wealth of the region that attracted the first Muslims to Central Asia but the drive to seek the pleasure of Allah by conveying the message of the ultimate truth; Al-Islam. The conquest of Central Asia and the implementation of Islam were completed in the eighth century CE. This process brought this region a "Belief" and culture that until now continues to

14 Ibn Rushd, *Bidayah al-Mujtahid*, Beirut, 1986, vol. I, p. 137.

15 Ibn Nadeem, *al-Fihrisht*, Cairo, vol. II, p. 118.

16 Abu Zuhra, *Hayat Abu Hanifa*, Delhi, 1978, p. 287.

17 Ibid., p. 588.

be dominant and overriding. The Muslims first entered Mawara al-Nahr in the middle of the seventh century through raids during their conquest of Persia. The Soghdians and other Iranian people of Central Asia were unable to defend their land against the *khilafah* because of internal divisions and the lack of strong indigenous leadership. The Muslims, on the other hand, were led by a brilliant general, Qutaybah bin Muslim, and were highly motivated by the desire to spread the Islamic ideology.

The new socio-religious and economic institutions brought by the Muslims revolutionized the local customary units and extended the chances for the cultural interaction throughout the region. The native cultures got replaced in the ensuing centuries as Islam moulded the people into a single force; the Islamic Ummah. However, the destiny of Central Asia as an Islamic region was firmly established by the Khilafah (Caliph Abu-al-'Abas) victory over the Chinese armies in CE 750 in a battle at the Talas River. Under Islamic rule, Central Asia was an important centre of culture and trade for centuries. The language of government, literature and commerce, originally Persian, became Arabic (however as the Abbasid caliphate began to weaken and Arabic became neglected, the Persian language began to regain its pre-eminent role in the region as the language of literature and government). Mawara al-Nahr continued to be an important political player in regional affairs. During the height of the Abbasid caliphate in the eighth and ninth centuries, Mawara al-Nahr experienced a truly golden age. The city of Bukhara became one of the leading centres of learning, culture and art in the Muslim world, its magnificence rivalling contemporaneous cultural centres such as Baghdad, Cairo and Cordova. Some of the greatest historians, scientists and geographers in the history of Islamic culture were natives of the region, and one of the copies of the Noble Quran (Quran al-Sharif) originally prepared in the time of Caliph 'Uthman has been kept in Tashqand.

The new Islamic spiritual and political situation in Central Asia determined a new technological and cultural progress. It marked the production of the Samarkand paper (since the eighth century under the Chinese influence the people of Samarkand learned to manufacture paper from the rags), which supplanted papyrus and parchment in the Islamic countries at the end of the tenth century. Furthermore, the scientists who were citizens of the *khilafah* such as al-Khwarizmi, al-Beruni, al-Farabi and Abu Ali bin Sina (Avicenna) brought fame to the area all over the world, generating respect across the world and many scientific achievements of the epoch made a great impact on the European science. It is pertinent to mention that the astronomical tables of Samarkand astronomers from Ulughbek's observatory had been under the consideration of Europian astronomers till eighteenth century CE. During the comparatively peaceful era of Islamic rule, culture and the arts flourished in Central Asia. The societal experiences at this stage were altogether different in comparison to the early Muslim society that experienced less interaction with the foreign cultures. The legal experts, at this moment, had to identify and respond to the façade of socio-cultural occurrences as well as to defend their argument with approved legal directives. The challenge of addressing this issue has been competently resolved and Muslim scholars rediscovered alternate legal methods, which did not confront the basic sources of the law. The jurists held the view that Quran and *Hadith* were not the "only" rather the basic and primary sources of legislation in Islam.[18] The sociality, itself came to be identified as a valid source of law and the jurists, at this moment, surpassed the traditionists who showed a bit stagnation regarding the alternate theories of legislation.

---

[18] K.M. Sheikh, *Hadith and Hadith Sciences*, Delhi, 2006, p. 161.

The deductive techniques and legal expertise of the Iraqi School of Law (Hanafi) flourished in Mawara al-Nahr during second/eighth century CE. The eminent disciples of Imam Abu Hanifa (d. AH 150), the founder of the Hanafi School of Islamic Law carried out this tremendous task. The vast region across the rivers Oxus and Jaxartes, what now is Central Asia, had been a predominant region of the Muslim caliphate of the Umayyad dynasty (CE 651–750) annexed to it by Qutaybah bin Muslim around CE 712-15. With the establishment and expansion of the Muslim rule, the scholars belonging to this region, showed utmost concern regarding the dissemination of the Islamic sciences. They had been firmly rooted and associated with the reputed scholars of Baghdad, Basra and Kufa. As a result they explored the legal expertise much efficiently than the traditionists of Mecca, Medina and Damascus. The legal treatises transmitted to this region opened a dynamic episode in the groundwork and formulation of the legal theory in Islam. The scholars and jurists of Central Asia consolidated diverse academic disciplines and added new dimensions to the Islamic jurisprudence.[19]

A general survey of the Islamic literature will narrate the splendid scholarship of the Central Asian literary figures in almost all the Islamic sciences. In the field of *tafsir* (Quranic exegesis), the renowned scholars including Jarullah Zamakhsheri (d. AH 467), Abu Bakr Razi (AH 513), Muhammad bin Abu al Fazl Bukhari (d. AH 418), Abu Bakr Qafal (d. AH 483), Abu Ishaq Maruzi (d. AH 318) and Ahmad bin Muhammad Farghani (d. AH 531) excelled and surpassed their contemporaries. The style of the Quranic exegesis presented by these scholars has been recognized all over the Muslim world and is identified highly competent, scholastic and rational in approach. A noteworthy feature of their deductions

---

[19] H.A.R. Gibb, *Arab Conquests in Central Asia*, New York, 1970, p. 62.

is the proper understanding of the language system and rational interpretation of revealed discourse. This verily has maintained the intellectual standards besides remaining loyal to the original sources.[20]

Similarly, in the field of *Hadith,* the scholars of this region contributed a commendable composition that has everlasting relevance. The grand traditionist, Muhammad bin Isma'il Bukhari (d. AH 256), compiled *Jami al-Sahih,* still believed next to the authority of Quran. Muslim bin Hajaj al-Qushayri al-Neshapuri (d. AH 264), authored *Sahih.* Abu 'Isa Muhammad al-Tirmizi (d. AH 279) presented *Jami.* Al-Nasai (d. AH 303) produced *Sunan.* Ibn Maja (d. AH 273) and Abu Dawoud (d. AH 275) also produced *Sunan* treatises in their own style. The scholars, from far off places, associated themselves with Central Asian scholars to meet out the exemplary standards of the literary criticism. In addition to this material, separate books concerning *Hadith* methodology appeared on the scene to glorify this respective field.[21]

The science of Islamic jurisprudence too has a deep-rooted, dynamic and vast history in Central Asia. During second–seventh centuries of AH (eight–thirteen centuries CE) the jurists of this region, debated over the alternate tools of law besides Quran and Sunnah. The Central Asian scholars, equipped with the deductive techniques of the Iraqi legal thought, thought much ahead of traditionist approach and made valuable contribution to the legal theory. During the Abbasid regime (CE 750–1258), the principal cities of Central Asia — Andijon, Bukhara, Farghana, Khiva, Samarkand, Shash, Merghinan, Merv, Neshapur, Osh, Tashqand and Tirmiz — were seats *par excellence.* The Abbasid rulers patronized the study of revealed

20 Tabakh al-Ragib, *Tarikh Afkar al-Ulum al-Islami,* Delhi, 1982, p. 107.

21 Tabakh al-Ragib, *Tarikh Afkar al-Ulum al-Islami,* Delhi, 1982, pp. 67-83.

and human sciences, and showed utmost concern regarding the discipline of Islamic jurisprudence. Thus, narrates Ibn Khalikan:

> From Baghdad to Bukhara, the most learned figures emerged and the science of Islamic jurisprudence remained widely acclaimed and preferred discipline in Islamic sciences.[22]

The development of a rich literary tradition in the field of Islamic jurisprudence dates back to the formative period of the legal thought that identified absolute methodologies to resolve things in conformity with the primary sources. As a much reliable system of religo-juridical thought, as Alfred von Kremer affirms,

> the highest and loftiest achievement of which Islam was capable.[23]

With ascension of the Abbasids to the caliphal throne in CE 750, scholarly and intellectual activities began to flourish throughout the Muslim lands. After consolidating the political and strategic fronts, the Abbasid rulers turned towards the intellectual, artistic and literary activities. The reign of the first two caliphs, Abu al-'Abas (CE 750-54) and Abu Ja'far Mansur (CE 754-75) consolidated the administrative front, while their successors drew considerations from scholastic and intellectual traditions of the world heritage. From the reign of fifth caliph Harun al-Rashid (CE 786) to the ninth, al-Wathiq (CE 842), the intellectual legacy attained the zenith of progress and Central Asian cities disseminated high academic pursuits in almost all the disciplines of Islamic learning.[24] The caliph Harun al-Rashid had tilt towards the study of legal discourse, logic and philosophy. These disciplines, as depicts their nature,

---

[22] Hallaq, op. cit., p. 62.

[23] P.K. Hitti, *History of the Arabs*, Macmillan, 2001, p. 398.

[24] Ibid., p. 399.

have much to share upon the basis of argument and analysis. This inclination was mainly due to the interaction with a variety of ethnicities and cultures that entered Muslim domains due to expansion and tolerant attitude. The situation demanded a logical and speedy disposal of various issues confronting the rulers and the legalists that time. Being masters of a vast and gigantic empire, the circumstances were altogether a big challenge for the Abbasids. They realized the fact that while ruling such a vast landmass, policies must be in accord with much realistic approach and eminent scholars are to be deployed to understand the socio-legal relationships. Islam now had become a world phenomenon and its legal system a genuine social accord where every verdict must have conformity from both revealed as well as rational standards. Abu Yusuf (AH 182) could realize all this and his engagement as Qazi al-Quzah (the Chief Justice) sustained the practical possibilities of Islamic legal order much efficiently. Thus, jurisprudence went all along the administration to attain socio-economic egaliterianism.[25]

Iraq, being the caliphal seat of the Abbasids, had been a prominent centre of the Hanafi School of Law. Abu Yusuf (AH 182), the distinguished disciple of Imam Abu Hanifa, preferred Hanafi jurists as *qazis* (judges) to various regional headquarters to bring legal uniformity throughout the Abbasid empire. It is in this context that a group of eminent jurists and legal experts was deputed to Mawara al-Nahr (Central Asia) to disseminate the precepts of the Hanafi School of Law to the native population.[26] Among the galaxy of Muslim jurists and legal theorists in Central Asia, we may mention Abu Bakr Maruzi (d. AH 211), the compiler of *al-Kafi*, Muhammad bin Maqatil al-Razi (d. AH 213), the compiler of *fatawa*, Muhammad

---

[25] N.J. Coulson, op. cit., p. 101.

[26] E.J. Brill and P.M. Holt, *The Cambridge History of Islam, UK*, 1953, vol. IV, pp. 318-20.

bin Shuj'a Balkhi (d. AH 266), who authored *Nawadir*, the grand jurist, Abu Laith Samarqandi (d. AH 321), compiler of *Kitab al-Nawazil* and several other treatises on the study of *hadith* and *fiqh*, Imam Zufr Balkhi (d. AH 362), author of *Masmu'at;* Muhammad bin 'Ali (d. CE 436), compiler of *Al-Mu'tamad fi Usul al-Fiqh;* 'Ali bin Abu Bakr Marghinani (d. AH 593), compiler of *Al-Hidayah;* 'Abd al-'Aziz bin Mazah (d. AH 536), compiler of *Fatawa al-Kubra;* Al-Nasafi (d. AH 537), author of *Al-Usul;* Abu Laith Nasr bin Muhammad bin Ahmad (d. AH 597), compiler of *Al-Majmu;* Muhammad bin 'Abd al-Rehman Maruzi (d. AH 533), author of *Al-Usul;* 'Uthman bin 'Ali Baqandi (d. AH 552), author of *Al-Usul al-Fiqh;* Bahauddin 'Ali bin Muhammad Samarkandi (d. AH 535), compiler of *Al-Mutamad* and Muhammad bin 'Abd al-Rehman Bukhari (d. AH 546), compiler of *Tafsir al-Quran* as men of highest stature.[27]

Due to the exertion and consolidation of these admired figures, the science of Islamic jurisprudence attained the elevated standards and could combat the Greek and the Roman tradition much effectively. The Central Asian jurists not only narrated the legal procedures and methodological doctrines but also tried to support their interpretations by sound argumentation. The Central Asian jurists not only refer the flow of information with regard to the discipline of Islamic jurisprudence, but also examined, evaluated and annotated the same to explore it for further explanations.[28]

The endeavour of compiling *shuruh* (annotation), *usul* (fundamentals), *rad* (refutation), *taqabul* (comparison), *tarjih* (preference), *talkhis* (synopsis), *tashrih* (explanation) and similar other celebal studies depicts the ardent curiosity of the scholars to make the discipline of Islamic jurisprudence relevant to the altering circumstances. The principle of *taghaur* (change) has

---

27 Ibn Khalikan, *Wafiyat al-Ayan*, Beirut, 1977, vol. III, p. 178.

28 A. Shalbi, *A History of Muslim Education*, Beirut, 1954, p. 143.

been explored and applied competently to figure out much appropriate deductions demonstrating the social context. *Abu Yusuf*'s (d. AH 182) *al-Rad 'ala Malik bin Anas, Ikhtilaf Abu Hanifa wa abu laila* and *Al-Rad ala siyr al-Auza'i* have been considered among the primary works compiled in this direction. Muhammad bin Hasan al-Shaybani's (d. AH 187) *Al-Rad 'ala ahl al-Medina* is also a masterpiece affirming the application of valid arguments while approaching the various sources of law.[29] Bazudi's (d. AH 482) *al-Usul*, Marghinani's (d. AH 593) *Mukhtarat al-fatawa*, Samarkandi's (d. AH 318) *Tuhfat-al fuqaha*, Farghani's (AH 419) *Nashr al-Madhahib* and Muhammad bin 'Ali's (AH 412) *al-Mu'tamad fi Usul al-Fiqh* are also the concrete materials that carry the methodological principles of alternate reasoning.[30] The material under reference has been consulted and utilized by the Central Asian jurists to inflate a variety of possible interpretations of a particular commandment (*hukm al-shara'i*).[31]

The study of Islamic jurisprudence got much impetus and incredible concern during the emergence of the sundry dynasties as well. When the Abbasid authority over Central Asia weakened, the Samanids took over as their succeeding authority. From AH 261/CE 873, the utmost portion of the Central Asian territory fell to the Samanids. The Samanids ascended the throne until AH 395/CE 1005 and were considered as the undisputed masters for a couple of centuries in the Central Asian region. The city of Bukhara remained the capital of the Samanid empire and a reputed centre for the dissemination of Islamic sciences.[32] Despite being the Amirs of Khurasan, the Samanids tried to unify all the

---

29 A. Shalbi, *A History of Muslim Education*, Beirut, 1954, p. 73.

30 T.W. Arnold and A. Guillaumme, *The Legacy of Islam*, Delhi, 1995, pp. 306-07.

31 Ibn Khalikan, op. cit., vol. III, pp. 188, 204.

32 D. Sinor, *The Cambridge of Early Inner Asia*, Britain, 1994, p. 347.

Central Asian regions through a uniform identity.[33] The inner core of the state was governed by various lieutenants appointed from the members of the dynasty.[34] The judicial procedures were made in accordance with the Shari'ah law and the judicial administration had been organized systematically. To them is attributed the magnificent tradition of the "Perso-Islamic legacy", a hallmark in the literal and artistic legacy of Islam.[35]

The reign of Samanid ruler Nasr-II (CE 913-42) had been no less significant, as it re-oriented scholars to make juristic deductions in the light of literature available as well as realizing the circumstances. It is due to his academic endeavour that noteworthy developments took place. He established grand libraries around his domain to study and facilitate the endeavour of Islamic sciences. The study and patronage to the science of Islamic jurisprudence had been among his privileged academic tastes.[36] He is also being credited with the zeal of compiling the scattered material on varied disciplines and establishing a grand library at Bukhara. This library contained the treatises on history, philosophy, Quranic exegeses, *Hadith*, medicine, logic and Islamic jurisprudence.[37] Ibn Sina (CE 980–1037), a renowned philosopher and scientist, while visiting this library admitted:

> Nasr's library at Bukhara contains valuable collections on almost all the branches of knowledge and has no parallel in Mawara al-Nahr.[38]

---

33 Narakhshi, *Tarikh-i-Bukhara*, tr. R.N. Frye, Cambridge, 1954, p. 84.

34 Ibid., p. 74.

35 Sinor, op. cit., p. 346.

36 Ibid., p. 348.

37 S. Saulat, *Milat-i-Islamiya ki Mukhtasar Tarikh*, 1994, Delhi, vol. I, pp. 244-45.

38 Ibn Khalikan, op. cit., vol. IV, p. 137.

The famous biographer and historian, Ibn Khalikan records:

> Some treatises (at Nasr's) *khazinah al-kutb* (library) are so rare that they were hardly to be traced anywhere else.[39]

The Samanids are very much remembered for the astonishing zeal of expanding Islam towards the eastward directions. The high administrative, judicial and literary standards proved their governance over the steppe. It is during this tenure that a huge number of the Central Asian tribes went over to Islam. The Turks, who are an identity of Islam in Central Asia, were converted during the reign of Samanids. We are told in the sources that it was the first interaction of the Turks to monitor Islam so intimately.[40] The renowned historians, Ibn Miskawiah and Ibn Athir, narrated that in the year CE 960, 2,00,000 tenants of Turks went over to Islam.[41] Subsequently, from CE 1043, 10,000 tenets of the Turks living between the provinces of Balasaghun and Bhagar accepted Islam.[42] The newly-converts to Islam in the steppe were identified as the tribes of Karakhanids and Illkhanids, who afterwards ascended the throne of Central Asian steppe. The *sūfī* missionaries who dived deep into the local tradition also made a valuable contribution regarding the service to Islam. They strengthened the social fabric by propagating the universal teachings of Islam in an uncomplicated way. The scholars and jurists were deputed to various regions of the steppe to acquaint the people regarding the understanding of Islam.[43]

One of the noteworthy developments during the Samanid period (CE 873–1005) is the diffusion and transmission of the

---

39 Ibn Khalikan, op. cit., vol. IV, p. 138.

40 Ibn Miskawiah, *Tajrub al-Umam*, Cairo, 1932, vol. I, p. 172.

41 Ibid., p. 172.

42 J. Kunitz, *Dawn Over Samarkand*, Calcutta, 1943, p. 118.

43 Saulat, op. cit., p. 244.

Islamic sciences in Persian language. The literature compiled in various disciplines up to this period had for the first time an opportunity to transmit the intellectual legacy beyond Arab lands. The process of transmission made an easy access to Islamic literature and encouraged scholars to produce their writings into the local languages. The reign of Nasr-II (CE 913-43) is considered dynamic as it empowered intellectual activities to attain the zenith of progress. The Samanids excelled in almost all the directions of artistic, intellectual and cultural aspects and extended their domain to its greatest limits including Sijistan, Kirman, Jurjan, Rai and Tabaristan in addition to Mawara al-Nahr and Khurasan. They professed loyalty to Abbasids of Baghdad but were independent, and their authority was undisputed.[44] The Samanids had a quest to transmit Islam into Central Asian and Persian traditions. The Arabic language, however, did not suffer. It remained the source of instruction and an imperative medium to approach the original sources of Islam. Apart from the compilations and treatises on Islamic jurisprudence, the renowned *magnum opus* of Ibn Jarir al-Tabari (d. CE 983), *Tarikh al-Rusul wa al-Muluk* and *Tafsir al-Tabari* were translated into Persian.[45] The works of al-Farabi (d. CE 918) on philosophy, Ibn Sina's (d. CE 1037) on science and medicine, Matrudi's (d. CE 942) on scholastic discourses and Abu Nasr Saraj's (d. CE 988) on mystic thought were also translated into Persian language.[46]

It is reported through the narratives of the reputed geographers Ishtakhri (d. CE 950), Maqdisi (d. CE 1072) and Ibn Hawqal (d. CE 977) that the Samanid cities throughout Khurasan and Turkistan were considered as the prestigious

---

44 Hitti, op. cit., p. 462.

45 S. Saulat, op. cit. p. 170, also see Maarif, Delhi, 1984, vol. 134, pp. 352-53.

46 Saulat, op. cit., p. 172

centres of agriculture, dexterity, commerce and learning.[47] The cities Samarkand, Bukhara, Merv and Neshapur were worldwide famous for literary men, skilled artisans and libraries. The private libraries of the Samanid rulers contained grand and superb collections on religion and philosophy.[48] The venture of intellectual and socio-cultural atmosphere in central Asia has been instantly narrated by al-Maqdisi (d. CE 1072):

> The people under the Samanid rule enjoy liberty. Crimes are not committed openly. The network of *madrasas* (seminaries) links together the entire region of Mawara al-Nahr. Samarkand is famous for the manufacturing of paper, land is fertile and shops and granaries are full of stock. Neshapur is the cradle of learning; scholars from far off places visit its libraries. Balkh is really the paradise of Khurasan. Rai is clean and beautiful. Bukhara is known as Qubat al-Islam (Identity of Islam). The cities, Khurasan, Herat and Merv are prestigious seats of learning and scholars of various disciplines are seen here.[49]

After the collapse of the Samanid rule in CE 1005, Central Asia fell to Khwarizm Shahs, Ghaznavids and Seljuk Turks until CE 1258. These local dynasties came to power due to internal disturbances and as the *'ulama* reasoned, were also Muslims, and hence, if that were God's will also worth of rule.[50] During this period the Central Asia and Persia were known for the artistic, intellectual and architectural patterns. The reign of Seljuk Turks had been prolific *vis-à-vis* the establishment of political and academic institutions. The science of Islamic

---

47 Al-Maqdisi, *Ahsan al-Taqasim fi Marifah al-Aqalim*, Cairo, AH 1370, p. 221.

48 Ibid., p. 223.

49 Ibid., p. 221.

50 Narakhshi, op. cit., p. 100.

jurisprudence observed a dynamic interest by both, the rulers as well as the scholars. The learned jurists of this era taught methodologies of *fiqh* throughout Central Asia, which later on have been brought to the Indian subcontinent even before the Mughal invasion of CE 1526.[51]

Islamic sciences in Central Asia got impetus and superb momentum with the engagement of Nizam al-Mulk Tusi (AH 400/CE 1048) as the grand vizier of the Seljuk's. He planned the restructure of the Islamic education system and had a zeal for the promotion of knowledge. To him is attributed the establishment of a network of religious seminaries throughout the Muslim lands. Moreover, he initiated a campaign of patronizing the scholars to promote the intellectual rehabilitation. The study of all the schools of law was carried out in a systematic manner. Being himself a prolific writer, he compiled *Dastur al-Wuzara* and *Siyasat Namah* two monumental treatises in the field of political science.[52] Imam Subki, a renowned religious scholar, considers him among the great reformists who contributed an immense share and influenced the world of Islam for centuries together.[53] The Nizami curriculum of the religious seminaries of Central Asia, Persia and Indian subcontinent is the brainchild of Nizam al-Mulk Tusi. The Hanafi *fiqh* methodology is a dominant factor in this curricula and it shaped the future discourse for the promotion of the Hanafi adherents all over the world. The Seljuk period of the Central Asian history is a marvellous chapter regarding the development of Islamic sciences as well as for the sponsorship of the Persian language and literature. The translation of the Arabic works especially on philosophy, poetry, Islamic jurisprudence, grammar and logic is still

51 A.S.K. Najibabadi, *Tarikh-i-Islam*, 1987, Delhi, vol. III, p. 318.

52 Tajuddin Subki, *Taqabat Shafiyah al-Kubra*, Cairo, vol. III, p. 218.

53 Ibid., p. 117.

attributed to the Seljuk Turks. The renowned poets' M'uizi (CE 1108), Anwari (CE 1126), Nizami (CE 1202) and Khaqani (CE 1185) enriched the Persian language along the valuable additions.[54]

Among the renowned theologians, jurists and philosophers of the Seljuk era, we may mention al-Ghazali (d. AH 505/CE 1111), 'Umar Khayam (d. AH 526/CE 1132), 'Abd al-Qadir Jilani (d. AH 561/CE 1166), Jalal-u-din Rumi (d. AH 672/CE 1294), Jaru Allah Zamakhsheri (d. AH 538/CE 1144), Shahristani (d. AH 548/CE 1153), 'Abdullah Ansari (d. AH 481/CE 1088) and Khazini (d. AH 516/CE 1122).[55]

The intellectual and scholarly activities of the Muslim world confronted a setback with the Genghis Khan's (CE 1162–1227) invasion of Central Asia in CE 1220. It proved much noxious as well as devastating. His grandson Halagu carried out the same attempt in CE 1258 and destroyed major part of the Muslim world along the destruction of the Abbasid capital Baghdad. Jalal-u-din Shah (CE 1220-31), a Khwarizmshahi monarch, showed some resistance but could not control the situation. The Mongol army destroyed the major Central Asian cities including Samarkand, Bukhara, Khwarizm, Balkh, Neshapur and Herat. The academic and intellectual structures of the Central Asian Muslim legacy were flattening to the ground. At least 2,000,000 Muslims were put to sword. The Mongol tribal chief Halagu in CE 1258 crossed the Oxus, creating havoc, entered the Abbasid capital Baghdad. After devastating every existing thing, murdered the Caliph Musta'sim (CE 1242-58) along with his 300 officials. The Mongols plundered city after city and thus ended a magnificent chapter of the Muslim history in Central Asia, Persia and Iraq. Finally, the Mamluk army of Egypt defeated the Mongols in CE 1260 at 'Ain Jalut and their advance towards westward direction was stopped.[56]

---

[54] Saulat, op. cit., vol. I, pp. 269-84.

[55] Haji Khalifah, *Kashf al-Zanun*, Istanbul, 1941, vol. III, p. 212.

[56] Hitti, op. cit., pp. 486-87.

2

Review of the Source Material

THE history of the juristic literature of Islam can be traced to the formative period that provided the basis for the study of various *'ulum* (disciplines) and broadened the ideological spectrum of Islam to formulate a compact knowledge system. Within the spectrum of revealed and socio-ethical codes, the discipline of Islamic jurisprudence emerged as a comprehensive and vast study to deduct and finalize the legal discourse from the basic and alternate sources of the law. As such, the science of Islamic jurisprudence denotes the accurate knowledge of the legal precepts passed on by Prophet Muhammad (SAW) to the forthcoming generations. The first three centuries of the Islamic era CE 632–950, are significant as well as illustrative. During this period, the literary and intellectual dynamism of Islam came to be recognized all over the world. The scholastic and socio-ethical system attained incredible loftiness and the political institutions depicted much comprehensive and mature set-up. The juristic literature in Islam has a magnificent history throughout centuries in which the Central Asian share is much gorgeous.

The sources pertaining to the study and history of the Islamic intellectualism in Central Asia cover and bring together a brilliant account of socio-cultural as well as political situation that paved the way for introducing Islamic traits. Historically speaking, in the first three centuries of the Islamic era Arabic remained as the language of all learning and knowledge throughout the lands which came under the extent of the Muslim territories. No wonder, therefore, in these centuries the sources are mainly in Arabic. Most prominent among them are *Ta'rikh al-Rusul wa al-Muluk* of Abu J'afar Muhammad bin Jarir al-Tabari (d. 310/CE 923) which was brought down to AH 302, and *Al-Kamil fi 't-Ta'rikh* of Izz al-Din Abul Husain 'Ali bin Muhammad ibn-al-Athir (d. AH 630) which was brought down to the year AH 628. Interestingly, Ibn al-Athir's work was published before that of al-Tabari.

It was only with the publication of Ibn al-Athir's work that the students of the history of Muslim East could feel themselves on firm ground. With the best possible care and greatest conscientiousness, almost a Utopia in those days, the author collected the material of different and diverse shades. Ibn al-Athir lays before us the actual figures of the personalities involved and also presents actual view of the prevailing circumstances both in administrative setup as well as in the society.

For the history of the first three centuries of Islam, Ibn al-Athir's chief source itself is *Tarikh* of al-Tabari. But the seniority of al-Tabari's work never lessens the importance of Ibn al-Athir's one. It retains an outstanding place amongst original sources, even for the history of the most ancient period of Islam. Ibn al-Athir deals with the material at his disposal with greater understanding. Quite often his sources remain inaccessible to us but again wherever we are in a position to verify his sources, we get results that favour Ibn al-Athir as the most authentic historian. This comparative study makes us to trust the author even without looking at his sources. The proof of this statement can be had from the following examples produced by Brockleman who has critically evaluated the authenticity of Ibn al-Athir. "It is only Ibn al-Athir who mentioned the conflicts between Chinese and Arabs in CE 751", which decided the fate of the western part of Central Asia as part of the Muslim East. Al-Tabari's work and all earlier historical works of Arabs are silent about this episode. However, Ibn al-Athir's mention of the event is perfectly corroborated by the Chinease history of the Tang dynasty.

In addition to the above mentioned works by al-Tabari and Ibn al-Athir, we have equally benefited among other later Arabic histories of importance, from the biographical dictionary *Wafiyyat al A'yan* of Shams al-Din Ahmad bin Muhammad Ibn-i-Khalikhan (d. 681/CE 1282). The first English edition of the book was published from Paris during CE 1842-71. The author enriches our information with the sources that have not come down to us before. Another important Arabic source with us is the famous universal history of Wali al-Din Abu Zayd 'Abdur-Rehamn ibn Khaldun (d. 808/CE 1406), the book, generally known as *Muqaddima,* was published at Bulaq in 1284/CE 1867. The author who lived in Spain and Africa has less to tell about Central Asia and still whatever little he says about Central Asia is present in Ibn al-Athir's work on whom the former has often relied. In agreement to the criticism of his contemporaries for his non-authenticity and irresponsibility, we find certain facts in *Muqaddima* which are in the first place not found in Ibn al-Athir and which again do not stand by the test of objectivity.

Apart from the bibliographical dictionaries and "Diwans", we have fairly a vast number of works — historical and literary — at our disposal especially towards the end of Umayyad period (CE 661–750). The diffusion of culture under Abbasids (CE 750–1258) resulted in the development of all branches of knowledge toward the end of tenth century CE. Abu al-Farj Muhammad bin Ishaq al-Nadim had to name his vast bibliographic work as *Fihrist al-'Ulum* (Index of the Sciences). This book provides some rare information about the scholars and branches of knowledge. We also find the names of Arab historians, which otherwise are nowhere known to us, in the *Muruj al-dahab wa M'adin al-Jawahar* (Golden Meadows) of

Abdul Hasan Ali bin Husain al-Mas'udi (d. 345/CE 956) published during CE 1861-77.

In addition to this source material, the following treatises also provide the relevant information on the legal discourse in Central Asia. To make a brief analysis of this particular study, we need to discuss some major relevant source materials, which formed the basis for the study of Islamic jurisprudence in Central Asia. In its formative period, the compilations and authoritative works of second and third century AH/eighth and ninth century CE have played a significant role.[1]

Introduction of the Juristic Compilations in Central Asia

The disciples of Imam Abu Hanifa (d. 150), the founder of Hanafi School of Law, or commonly known as "Fuqaha al-Draq" (the jurists of Iraq) did a commendable effort. The Iraqi Muslim jurists during eighth century CE are lead responsible for the introduction of juristic treatises in Central Asia. The interaction with the compilations and manuscripts of the early jurists of second and third century AH opened a magnificent chapter of Islamic jurisprudence in Central Asia. This exersion and involvement formed the basis for a rich literary tradition for dissemination of the Islamic sciences in the entire region. After being annexed to the caliphate by Qutaybah bin Muslim during CE 712-15, the chief vicinities of this region emerged as centres for acquisition and dissemination of the Islamic sciences. As the Islamic civilization flourished and expanded, or later some powerful Muslim dynasties sprang up and royal authority increased and stable administration maintained a high standard of law and order particularly in the chief cities and towns, sciences were cultivated, books were written,

[1] Haji Khalifah, *Kashf al-Zunun*, Beirut, 1953, pp. 2021-23.

copied, translated and transcribed in large number. In this learned venture, the Muslims were having a decent settlement, i.e. they had learnt the art of manufacturing paper from the Chinese as early as CE 751. The famous city Samarkand has the pride of establishing the first paper-making industry in the Muslim world.[2] Narrating the venture and process of dissemination of Islamic sciences in medieval Central Asia, a contemporary scholar Zia-ul-Hassan Faruqi comments:

> Consequently, this process helped and made easy according to the contemporary standard, the establishment of libraries generally known as *khizanat-al-kutab*. Along with this development, the craft of book production attracted the attention of not only scholars but patrons of learning and the learned also. . . . This historical development paved the way for the quickening of writing activity and the establishment of libraries throughout the Islamic lands and Samarkand became famous and widely known for its paper. This city remained a centre of learning for a long time and was the capital of the great empire that Timur (CE 1369–1404) had built up.[3]

The libraries of Samarkand, Bukhara, Ghaznah, Baghdad, Herat, Marv, Balkh, Tus, Neshapur and Shiraz had grand collections of *tafsir* (commentaries of Quran), *Hadith* (prophetic traditions), *fiqh* and *usul al-fiqh* (science of Islamic jurisprudence). Likewise the cities Tashqand, Andijon, Shash, Farghana, Marghinan, Khiva and Tirmiz possessed public, semi-public and private libraries for academic consultation. These libraries contained distinguished material particularly in the field of Islamic jurisprudence.[4]

The teachings of the Iraqi School of Islamic jurisprudence

---

[2] Narakhshi, *Tarikh-i-Bukhara*, Tashqand, 1897, p. 196.

[3] M. Taher, *Islamic Institutions*, Delhi, 1988, pp. 107-09.

[4] Ibid., p. 112.

lead by the pioneers like 'Abdullah bin Mas'ud, 'Alqamah (d. AH 62), Masruq (d. AH 63), al-Aswad bin Yazid (d. AH 75), Shuraih bin Harith (d. AH 75), Abrahim-al-Nakh'i (d. AH 96), Sh'abi (d. AH 103), Hammad bin Salma (d. AH 120), Abu-Hanifa (d. AH 150) and his disciples like Abu Yusuf (d. AH 182), Muhammad bin Hasan al-Shaybani (d. AH 189) and Imam Zufr (d. AH 158) had already been introduced to build much effective legal alliance with Baghdad. With the appointment of Qazi Abu Yusuf (d. AH 182) as the chief *qazi* of 'Abbasid caliphate, the legal and juridical impressions in Central Asia resembled the character of Baghdad in both, letter and spirit. Qazi Abu Yusuf appointed and preferred Hanafi *qazi*s and jurists for different provinces to settle the issues regarding socio-religious importance. The appointment of Abu Yusuf as chief *qazi* proved much beneficial for the introduction of Hanafi School of Law in Mawara al-Nahr. Ibn-al-Barr treats his service as the most valuable appointment in the 'Abbasid regime.[5]

COMPILATIONS OF IMAM ABU YUSUF

Imam Abu Yusuf (d. AH 182) was the most distinguished and gifted disciple of Imam Abu Hanifa. He is credited and associated with the work of introducing the Hanafi School of Thought in medieval Central Asia. His most celebrated work, *Kitab-al-Kharaj* published in Egypt in AH 1382 provides even the minute details of revenue, production, resources, treasury and treatment of legal issues during the Abbasid period. Besides *Kitab-al-Kharaj*,[6] Abu Yusuf compiled the following books: *Kitbal-al-Aasar, Ikhtilaf-Abu-Hanifa-wa-Abi-Laila, Kitab-al-Salat, Kitab-al-Zakat, Kitab-al-Siyam, Kitab-al-Faraiz, Kitab-al-Bayu, Kitab-al-Hudud, Kitab-al-Wakalah, Kitab-al-Wasaya, Kitab-al-Sayad-wa-Zibayah, Kitab-al-Ghazb-wa-al-Istibra, Kitab-al-Ikhtilaf-al-Amsar, Kitab-al-Radd-ala-Malik bin Anas, Kitab-al-Jawami* and *al-Radd-Ala-*

[5] Ibn al-Barr, *Al-Intiqa*, Cairo, AH 1350, p. 172.

[6] Abu Yusuf, *Kitab al-Kharaj*, Salfia, Egypt, AH 1352, p. 45.

Siyar-al-Awza'i. These reputed compilations formed the basis for the development of Hanafi School of Law in Mawara al-Nahr.[7]

JURISTIC COMPILATIONS OF IMAM MOHAMMAD BIN HASSAN-AL-SHAYBANI

Imam Muhammad bin Hassan al-Shaybani (AH 132-89) is another prominent figure whose compilations played a crucial role regarding the introduction of Hanafi School of Law in this region. The credit of compiling books on *usul al-fiqh*, discourses of *A'ima Mujtahidin*, and books on systematic legal reasoning is the legal venture of Mohammad bin Hassan Shaybani. His systematic legal thought and reasoning are primarly based on Quran and Sunnah, which he regards the basic sources of Islamic legal discourse. The contemporary historian of the Islamic legal thought and *usul al-fiqh*, W.B. Hallaq holds:

> It was Mohammad bin Hassan al-Shaybani who incited for the first time that no legal ruling can be valid unless it is based upon a binding text, by which he meant the Quran and the Prophetic traditions, although reports of the companions (*sahaba*), still played some role in his doctrine.[8]

Mohammad bin Hassan al-Shaybani's compilations have been considered as the source of inspiration and much authentic material for the introduction of Hanafi School of Law in Central Asia. Shaybani (d. AH 189) was a prominent disciple of Imam Abu Hanifa and Imam Abu Yusuf whom he considers as the masterminds regarding the formulation of the Islamic legal system. Shaybani's works have been authenticated and considered to be the hallmark in the socio-legal framework.

---

[7] Ibn Nadeem, *Al-Fihrist*, Cairo, AH 1348, pp. 286-88.

[8] W.B. Hallaq, *A History of Islamic Legal Theories*, Cambridge, 1997, p. 18.

These works if employed efficiently can prove vital to the study of legal methodologies in the contemporary Islam. The scholars of Bukhara, Samarkand, Asbahan, Shiraz, Jurjan, Tus, Marghinan, Farghana, Shash and Neshapur validiate his legal thought and try to conform their understanding and viewpoint through Shaybani's works.[9]

Shaybani's compilations have been preserved in the *kutub khana* (library) of Nuh bin Mansur (CE 976-97) a great monarch and a patron of arts and literature. This *kutub khana* is situated in Bukhara and is famous for enormous collections on *fiqh* literature, arts and sciences. As far as *fiqh* literature is concerned, it possessed books compiled by most predominant figures and legal doctors up to eleventh century CE. The Central Asian Muslim scholars have great influence and respect for the compilations of Shaybani. His juristic works were introduced in this region and in a short span of time his scholarship flourished and encouraged the venture of exploring the doctrines of Hanafi School of Law in almost all the chief vicinities of Central Asia.[10] The Central Asian scholars of Islamic jurisprudence have utilized Shaybani's works as the basic source material regarding the formulation of legal precepts. His foremost works on Islamic jurisprudence have been classified into, "Zahir al-Riwayah" and "Gair Zahir al-Riwayah".[11]

Zahir al-Riwayah

Shayabani's juristic works entitled Zahir al-Riwayah consist of the following six books: 1. *Al-Mabsut*; 2. *Al-Ziyadat*; 3. *Al-Jami-al-Sagir*; 4. *Al-Jami-al-Kabir*; 5. *Al-Siyar-al-Sagir*; and 6. *Al-Siyar-al-Kabir*.

[9] Gangohi, *Zafr al-Muhasilin*, Deoband: Hanief Book Depot, India, 1996, p. 655.

[10] Ibn Nadeem, op. cit., p. 290.

[11] Abu Zuhra, *Hayat Abu Hanifa*, Urdu tr. Hariri, Delhi: Itiqad Publishing House, 1978, p. 380.

These works serve as the basic reference material regarding the Hanafi School of Law in Islam. While authoring the compilations on Islamic jurisprudence, the Muslim scholars chiefly rely upon these works due to their socio-legal content and absolute juristic approach.

Gair Zahir-al-Riwayah

Gair Zahir-al-Riwayah consists of five juristic compilations: 1. *Kaysaniyat*; 2. *Haruniyat*; 3. *Jurjaniyat*; 4. *Al-Ruquyat*; and 5. *Ziyadat-al-ziyadat*.

The Gair Zahir-al-Riwayah is consulted when a proper and reliable discourse, verdict or legal resemblance is not found in the books entitled "Zahir-al-Riwayah".

Although Shaybani's works represent a particular juristic school of thought, still other schools of law in Islam refer to his works as *magnum opus* in the entire corpse of the literature in Islamic jurisprudence. This is indeed the first intellectual attempt to write on the legal instruments and their efficacy which in fact contributed a lot to the cultivation of Islamic jurisprudence in its formative phase.

COMPILATIONS OF HASSAN BIN ZIYAD

Imam Hassan bin Ziyad's (d. AH 204) compilations played a significant role in Islamic jurisprudence. He is among the reliable disciples and famous narrators of Abu Hanifa's legal discourses. He has narrated *Kitab-al-Mujjarad* which is attributed to Imam Abu Hanifa. He was appointed chief *qazi* of Kufa in AH 194 who transmitted *fiqh* methodology to far off areas of the caliphate in order to bring unity and legal integrity in the Abbasid empire. His thought and renowned scholarship are evident through his following works: 1. *Kitab-al-Adab-al-Qazi;* 2. *Kitab-al-Khasal;* 3. *Kitab-al-Aiman;* 4. *Kitab-al-Nafaqat;* 5. *Kitab-al-Kharraj;* 6. *Kitab-al-Faraiz;* and 7. *Kitab-al-Wasaya.*

The contemporary renowned Egyptian scholar Abu-Zuhra holds the view that his juristic compilations have been utilized as the basic source and reference material by Hanafi jurists of Iran and Mawara-al-Nahr for the study and conformation of the legal discourse.[12]

JURISTIC WORKS OF 'ISA BIN ABAN

Imam 'Isa bin Aban (d. AH 220) was a famous and versatile disciple of al-Shaybani. He was appointed as chief *qazi* of Basrah where he served for a long time. The Hanafi jurists of medieval era utilized his deductive legal methods of preference and analogy while conforming and supporting the Islamic legal theory. While deducing laws from commonly accepted methods of juristic preference, 'Isa bin Aban's juristic contribution is crucial as well as reliable. The renowned biographer Ibn Nadeem credits him with the following works: 1. *Kitab-al-Hajj;* 2. *Kitab-al-Khabar-al-Whid;* 3. *Kitab-al-Jami;* 4. *Kitab-al-Isbat-al-Qiyas;* and 5. *Kitab-al-Ijtihad-al-Rai.*[13]

JURISTIC WORKS OF MUHAMMAD BIN SAMA'AH

Imam Muhammad bin Sama'ah (d. AH 233) was a gifted disciple of Imam Muhammad bin Hassan al-Shaybani and Hassan bin Ziyad. The Abbasid caliph Mamun (CE 833) appointed him as *qazi* in AH 192. He established special courts for decrees regarding the much-complicated issues to get the maximum possibilities while dealing with any particular issue. *Kitab-al-Adab-al-Qazi* and *Kitab-al-Muhazar*[14] are among his famous works that deal with the fundamentals of judiciary.

JURISTIC WORKS OF HILAL BIN YEHYA-AL-BASRI

The grand jurist, Imam Hilal bin Yehya (d. AH 245) was no less

---

[12] Abu Zuhra, op. cit., p. 380.

[13] Ibid., p. 382.

[14] Ibid., p. 382.

significant. He is considered as the authority regarding *auqaf*. Ibn Nadeem has not mentioned his works in *al-fihrist* but Abu-Zuhra treats him as authority in Islamic juristic thought and attributes to him two compilations *Kitab-al-Tafsir-al-Shurut* and *Kitab-al-Hudud*.[15]

Juristic Works of Ahmad bin 'Umar bin Muhair-al-Khasaf

Ahmad bin 'Umar bin Muhair-al-Khasaf (d. AH 261) was predominant among the jurists of third century AH. His works were utilized by Central Asian jurists of the medieval times. Ahmad bin 'Umar's *Kitab-al-Auqaf* serves as reference material regarding the laws of trusts and appropriations. Besides *Kitab-al-Auqaf* he has compiled the following books: 1. *Kitab-al-Hiyal;* 2. *Kitab-al-Wasaya;* 3. *Kitab-al-Shurat-al-Kabir;* 4. *Kitab-al-Shurat-al-Saghir;* 5. *Kitab-al-Raza;* 6. *Kitab-al-Muhazir;* 7. *Kitab-al-Adab-al-Qazi;* 8. *Kitab-al-Khawarij;* 9. *Kitab-ul-Qasr-wa-Ahkam;* and 10. *Kitab-al-Samer-wa-al-Qabr.*[16]

JURISTIC COMPILATIONS OF IMAM TAHAVI

Imam Ahmad bin Muhammad Tahavi (d. AH 321) is regarded as the scholar *par excellence*. His juristic approach has been endorsed by various schools of Islamic jurisprudence and itself considered as a separate school of law. He was an extraordinary commentator, a renowned traditionist and above all a great jurist. He has done a marvellous contribution almost in all the branches of Islamic religious sciences. He acquired his knowledge by travelling to distant areas and learned jurisprudence from Abu-Hazam Abdul Hamid, the chief *qazi* of Syria, who was among the renowned disciples of 'Isa bin Aban.

Imam Tahavi's compilations constitute profound doctrines

---

15 Abu Zuhra, op. cit., p. 388.

16 Al-Qarshi, *Al-Jawahar al-Muziah*, Hyderabad, AH 1332, vol. I, p. 178.

of the legal thought that helped in the growth of Islamic jurisprudence as well as in the constitution of the legal theory. They reflect the lofty modes of interpretation and have been considered much appropriate and logical in the Islamic social and legal precepts. His contribution to the diverse branches of religious sciences ranks him as the *mujtahid* of first category. His works in the Islamic sciences include: 1. *'Ahkam-al-Quran;* 2. *Kitab-al-Maani-al-Aasar;* 3. *Mushkil-al-Aasar;* 4. *Al-Mukhtasar;* 5. *Sharah-al-jama Saghir;* 6. *Sharah-al-jama-Kabir;* 7. *Kitab-al-shurat-al-Kabir-wa-Saghir;* 8. *Kitab-al-Ausat;* 9. *Al-Muhazir-wa-Sijilat;* 10. *Al-Wasaya-wa-al-Faraiz;* 11. *Hukm-al-Arazi-al-Makkah;* and 12. *Qasm-al-Fai-wa-al-Ghanaim.*[17]

This contribution had been very much significant and was carried to the vast regions of the caliphate to serve the objective of socio-legal reforms.

Sources Pertaining to the Study of Islamic Jurisprudence in Central Asia

This illusterious account of the source material contains the works that have straight correlation with the study of Islamic legal thought in Central Asia. It will also anthologize the relevant material/biographies of reputed jurists associated with the development of Islamic jurisprudence up to the thirteenth century CE. The annotation of the same is produced here.

MUSNAD

The reputed treatise, *Musnad* is among the early compilations authored in the field of Islamic jurisprudence. It was compiled by Imam Abu Hanifa (d. AH 150), the founder of Hanafi School of Law. The work is based on the juristic interpretation of selected prophetic traditions narrated through the profound authority of reliable narrators. The book attempts over the

---

[17] Al-Lakhnawi, *Al-Fawaid al-Bahiah*, Lucknow, AH 1311, p. 18.

rulings from 532 prophetic traditions. Tayyib Library, Saharanpur, UP, India, has published its Indian edition in 1987. The book has been divided into thirty-three chapters and a topical heading separates each chapter as devised in the arrangement. The jurists, while compiling their works on jurisprudence, have acknowledged this treatise and utilized its methods of deduction for further legal advance. The work is considered among the primary sources regarding the history of the systematic legal reasoning in Islam.

The Central Asian Muslim scholars preferred *Musnad* to other juristic works mainly due to its power of the beauty of the analysis while deducing the laws pertaining to Shari'ah. Abu Hanifa, himself, narrates the prophetic traditions from the companions of the Holy Prophet (SAW) and justifies his viewpoint in the light of rational interpretation.

KITAB-AL-KHARAJ

Imam Abu Yusuf, to establish a systematic scheme of revenue as well as to ascertain the proper arrangement of resource distribution, compiled the *magnum opus*, *Kitab-al-Kharaj*. It is an undisputed, reliable and most authentic work authored for the treatment of fiscal and economic reforms. The jurists often refer this work as it carries information and description on the issues of revenue, treasury, production and utilization of the economic resources. The Anglo-Oriental Book Shop published it from Egypt in AH 1382. In the juristic works of the Central Asian scholars, *Kitab-al-Kharaj* remains the basic source while dealing with the disbursement of a variety of economic issues. The Abbasid caliph, Harun al-Rashid (CE 786) requested for its compilation and it emerged as the first treatise to deal with Islamic policy of revenue and land reform. Abu Yusuf attempts over the basic issues related to the revenue of productive/non-productive, agrarian/non-agrarian lands, and its treatment is provided by a sound, systematic and balanced interpretation.

AL-MUKHTASAR-AL-QUDOORI

Al-Mukhtasar-al-Qudoori was compiled by Abdul Hassan Ahmad bin Abu Bakr (d. AH 428). This work has remained in the course curricula of the Hanafi School of Law since its compilation. The medieval Islamic scholars of jurisprudence while compiling their works have benefited from this treatise and relied upon the methodology presented by the author. The style, *abwab* (scheme of chapterization) and explanation of the basic sources of law are scholarly concerns that have rendered a vital service to reorient the juristic explanations in a systematic manner. This book has always been a source of inspiration for the Muslim scholars to develop the juristic literature as well as to think for the alternate approaches of the legal methodology.[18]

KITAB-AL-HIDAYAH

The *magnum opus, Kitab-al-Hidayah* was compiled by Burhan-al-Din 'Ali-bin Abu Bakr Marghinani (d. AH 593). Navalkishore Press, in AH 1326, in two volumes, published its Indian edition. Charles Hamilton, the legal advisor to the British Governor-General in India, Warren Hastings produced its English translation (1773-76) in four volumes. This celebrated work consists of fifty-seven books concerning almost all the socio-economic, legal and political institutions of Islam. Since the work is first of its kind, it has been conformed as the basic treatise for Muslim Personal Law in Caucasus and South Asian British jurisdictions during the eighteenth century. The author being a native of Samarkand reviewed all the possible literature and attempted to produce a treatise of a much competitive stature. Its legal authority influenced the Central Asian scholars of Islamic jurisprudence as this celebrated work annotated almost all the legal interpretations in an analytical manner. It is the legal and socio-ethical implication of this work that Muslim scholars in every age tried to annotate

---

[18] Al-Lukhnawi, *Muqadimah al-Hidayah*, Delhi: Naval Kishore, AH 1312, p. 20.

its text to rediscover varied dimensions of the legal theory. Commentaries, especially in Arabic, Persian, Turkish and Urdu have been written to it to obtain the maximum possibilities for the understanding of the socio-religious discourse.[19]

AL-QAND FI-DHIKR 'ULAMA-I-SAMARKAND

Al-Qand fi-Dhikr 'Ulama-i-Samarkand was compiled by Najm-ud-din 'Umar bin Muhammad al-Nasafi. The book has been published by Maktaba-al-Kousar, Saudi Arabia, in 1987. It is an encyclopaedic work covering almost all the aspects of religious sciences contributed by the scholars of Samarkand and its adjacent provinces. The venture of this celebrated work is the special care of those literary figures who cultivated the Islamic intellectualism in Central Asia. The history of the transmission and dissemination of the *Hadith* and *fiqh* literature is an incredible facet of this reputed treatise.

KASHF-AL-ZANUN

Kashf-al-Zanun is among the most reliable encyclopaedic works ever authored in the history of Islam. The eminent Muslim historian and biographer Haji Khalifa compiled this work with utmost zeal to prepare a profound sketch of the Muslim scholars and reviewed their contribution in a much talented manner. The work has been published by Dar-al-Fikr, Beirut, Lebanon, in AH 1360. It is endowed with the information regarding the compilers of the Islamic social and religious sciences until thirteenth century AH.[20] It is a voluminous work with much authentic and reliable information about the venture of jurisprudence in Central Asia and other parts of the Muslim

---

19 A detailed account of the commentaries on al-Hidayah is in my M.Phil. dissertation, "A Critical Study of al-Farghani's Treatment of the Sources in al-Hidayah" submitted to The Centre of Central Asian Studies, The University of Kashmir, J&K, in 2004.

20 Haji Khalifah, op. cit., pp. 1830-52.

world. The second volume of this celebrated work has special relevance to this study as it provides a detailed account of the following:

1. A brief account of the juristic works compiled in Farghana, Merghinan, Bukhara, Samarkand and Neshapur.
2. Illustrated the life, works and approach of the reputed scholars of the various disciplines of the Islamic studies.

Being specific, Haji Khalifa has dealt more precisely while discussing the nature of some juristic treatises in certain parts of Central Asia. He has narrated the contribution of Uzbek jurists but has not evaluated the nature and role of these works for the development of legal theory in this region.

AL-JAWAHAR-AL-MUZIAH

Al-Jawahar-al-Muziah was compiled by 'Abd al-Qadir al-Qarshi. It was published in Egypt in AH 1343, its Indian edition was published by Dairat-al-Ma'arif, Hyderabad, in AH 1332. Al-Qarshi was a renowned scholar and famous disciple of Imam Marghinani (d. AH 539). Al-Qarshi has maintained the record of reputed jurists of Mawara al-Nahr in his Tazkirah. His role is no less significant as he holds the prominent position among the forerunners of Islamic jurisprudence in Central Asia. The book has special relevance with this study as it discusses works and biographies of prominent jurists of this region. Although al-Qarshi has narrated the venture of Islamic jurisprudence in a superb manner, he has not mentioned some towering scholars of the medieval Central Asia and Turkistan who decisively contributed to the codification of Islamic law in this region.

AL-A'ALAM

Al-A'alam is an encyclopaedic work compiled by Khayr-al-din Zarkali. Rehmania Press, Cairo, Egypt, in AH 1332, published its first edition. The author has paid special attention while dealing with the contribution of medieval Central Asian jurists and dealt with their methodology at length. The compiler, in volume V of this renowned work has mentioned a brief account of the jurists and scholars of Samarkand, Merghinan and Farghana. However the work is silent on their role in the socio-political and administrative scenario.[21]

AL-FIHRIST

Al-Fihrist holds a distinguished position within the encyclopaedic works of the Islamic studies. This masterpiece is the work of noted Muslim historian and biographer Ibn Nadeem Muhammad bin Ishaq, published by Rehmania Press, Cairo, in AH 1334. Volumes VI and VII of this work take a brief account of jurisprudence in the medieval Central Asia during the Abbasid regime.

WAFIYAT-U-AL A'YAN

Wafiyat-u-al-A'yan-wa-Anba-i-Abna-al-Zaman is an encyclopaedic work by Ibn Khalikan, published by Dar-al-Sadar, Beirut, Lebanon, 1977-78 in eight volumes. Volume 3 of this work makes a detailed description of the jurisconsults of the Hanafi School of Law in second and third century AH. The work also attempts to describe about the legal methodologies that resulted for the development of legal theory in Islam.

AL-FAWAID-AL-BAHIYYA

Muhammad Abu-al-Hai Lakhnavi compiled *Al-Fawaid-al-Bahiyya-fi-Tarajim-al-Hanafiyah*. This work has been published from Lucknow, India, in AH 1311 and mainly deals with the contribution of the Hanafi jurists of different times. The author has shown great concern to point out the works of well-versed scholars of medieval Central Asia and Iraq. In addition to this,

---

[21] Khair al-Din Zarkali, *Al-A'alam*, Cairo, AH 1332, vol. V, p. 418.

the author has compiled a valuable commentary on the source material of Burhan-ud-din 'Ali bin Abu Bakr's *Al-Hidayah*. In AH 1324 its second edition appeared from Cairo, Egypt. The aim being to introduce its methodology for the academic purpose in Egyptian colleges and universities. The reputed author of this work has not endorsed some towering jurists of Central Asia; however by a brief description, some of the juristic traditions have been acknowledged.

MUJAM-AL-MU'ALIFIN

Mujam-al-Mu'alifin is an encyclopaedic work that carries valuable information on the compilers of the Islamic sciences and their methodological approaches in the different aspects of Islamic learning. This *magnum opus* has been compiled by 'Umar Raza Kahalah and published by Dar-al-Ahya-al-Turath-al-Arabi from Beirut in 1959. The famous jurisconsults like Marghinani, Nasafi, Shashi and Qazi Khan along with their compilations have been entertained in volume VII of this reputed work. The treatise however remains silent about the socio-political occurrences at that time.[22]

HAYAT ABI-HANIFA

Hayat Abi-Hanifa was compiled by the renowned Egyptian luminary Sheikh Muhammad Abu Zuhra. He retired as a professor of law at Al-Fawad University, Egypt. The original Arabic text was published from Egypt and then translated into Urdu by Ghulam Ahmad Hariri, published by A'tiqad Publishing House, New Delhi, in 1987. Abu Zuhra's profound scholarship in Islamic jurisprudence has made this book a valuable academic venture. The scholar has critically examined the source material of the Hanafi School of Law that is considered to be the basic reference for juristic compilations in Central Asia and Iraq. It is to note that the chapters especially

[22] 'Umar Raza Kahalah, *Mujam al-Mualifin*, Beirut, 1969, vol. VII, pp. 167-79.

27, 30, 35, 41, 42, 55 and 62 have been consulted to establish a proper and balanced opinion regarding the judgement of the source materials attributed to second and third/eighth and ninth-century CE jurists. The author has made a valuable attempt to investigate into the nature of the Hanafi source material and examined the alternate theories of the Islamic law adopted by the Hanafi jurists.

BADAYA-AL-SANAYA-FI-TARTIB-AL-SHA'RAYA

Badaya-al-Sanaya-fi-Tartib-al-Sha'raya was compiled by 'Ala-ud-din Abu-Bakr bin Mas'ud-al-Kasani (d. AH 587), published by Dar-ul-Kutub-al-'Ilmiyah, Beirut. It is an exemplary commentary on *Tuhfat-al fuqaha* compiled by Samarkandi. *Badaya-al-sanaya* is one of the basic source materials which contains *tarjih* (the doctrines of preference) and the methods of deducing laws from the discourses of the companions and their successors. It approaches to the basic legal stuff and issues of the juristic preference, provides with the opinion of different schools of law, and provides the sound arguments in support of the Hanafi School of Law.

AL-FURUQ-AL-KARABISI

Al-Furuq-al-Karabisi was compiled by Asad bin Muhammad al-Neshapuri (d. AH 570), published by Wazarat-al-Auqaf-al-Kuwaitiyah, Lebenon. This book represents the juristic traditions of the forerunners of the Hanafi School of Law who added sound and reliable references to the Islamic legal theory. The compiler of this renowned book has not discussed opinion of the other schools of law, as Neshapur has always represented the Hanafi School of Islamic jurisprudence.

KASHF-AL-ASRAR SHARAH USUL-AL-BUZUDI

Kashf-al-Asrar Sharah Usul-al-Buzudi was compiled by 'Ala-ud-din 'Abdul 'Aziz bin Ahmad-al-Bukhari (d. AH 730), published by Dar-al-Kutub-al-Islamiyah, Beirut. The author gives a detailed account of the legal sources and doctrines of Islamic law identified by Imam Bazudi. Its preface provides a valuable description of the history of Islamic jurisprudence in Bukhara and other famous cities of Uzbekistan. The book has special relevance with the present study.

THE CAMBRIDGE HISTORY OF ISLAM

The Cambridge History of Islam edited by P.M. Holt, published by Cambridge University Press, London, UK, has compiled an article "Law and Justice" in volume 2B which narrates the history of juristic literature from various cities of Uzbekistan and Central Asia. This article has highlighted and discussed the source material on Islamic law during the Abbasid and Samanid periods.

ENCYCLOPAEDIA OF ISLAM

Encyclopaedia of Islam, vol. IV, edited by E.J. Brill, has given a list of prominent juristic commentaries compiled by the scholars of Central Asia and Uzbekistan. Some valuable references for chapter III have been entertained from this work. The nature and approaches of the compilations has not been discussed at length, however, the work is much valuable for the scholarly pursuits and general topics of Islamic studies.

THE CAMBRIDGE HISTORY OF IRAN

The Cambridge History of Iran, edited by William B. Fisher et al., published in 1968-69 in 7 vols. Volume IV, gives the list of the jurists and their contribution in the article "Jurisprudence and Its Principles". Volume IV, From Arab Invasion to Saljuks, edited by Richard Nelson Fyre (1975) and vol. V Saljuks and Mongol Periods, edited by John Andrew Boyle (1968), have been dedicated to the development and expansion of the Islamic institutions.

DAIRA-T-AL-MA'ARIF-AL-ISLAMIYA

Daira-t-al-Ma'arif-al-Islamiya, Danishgah-i-Punjab, Lahore, vol. 20, 9, 13, 17, contain the material on Islamic jurisprudence in medieval Transoxiania. Volume 20 of this encyclopaedia provides a brief description of the legal theoretical discourses in an explored form which has a special relevance with this study.

MA'ARIF

Ma'arif, vol. 134, October–November 1984, has published an article by 'Ubaydullah Koti Nadvi which provides a detailed description about the legal methods deployed to deduce laws from sources of Shari'ah. In this perspective he has mentioned medieval Central Asian and Uzbek scholars who performed valuable services in this respective field. The scholarly journal is being published from Dar-al-Mussanifin, Delhi.

TEHZIB-AL-TEHZIB

Tehzib-al-Tehzib, a renowned work in Islamic literature, has been compiled by Sheikh-al-Islam Ahmad bin Hajr-al-'Asqalani, second edition, 1993, by Maktaba-al-Beirut, acknowledges the contribution of Muslim jurists and gives valuable information about the juristic compilations of medieval Uzbekistan. Its Indian edition was published by Daira-al-Ma'arif, Hyderabad, in AH 1327.

A HISTORY OF ISLAMIC LEGAL THEORIES

A History of Islamic Legal Theories, authored by Wael B. Hallaq, published by Cambridge University Press in 1997, traces the origin, evolution and development of the Islamic legal theories from its beginning to the period of codification. This analysis includes a comprehensive account of the early formation of the theory, focusing on its main themes and enables us to understand its evolution/development in different periods of the Islamic history. The book is a valuable venture to examine the legal methodologies of the Sunni schools of Islamic jurisprudence.

ZAFR-AL-MUHASILIN-FI-AHWAL-AL-MUSANIFIN

Zafr-al-Muhasilin-fi-Ahwal-al-Musanifin, compiled by Maulana Muhammad Haneef Gangohi, published by Haneef Book Depot, Saharanpur, UP (India), contains the biographies of the famous jurists including the scholars of Central Asia and medieval Uzbekistan. The second volume attached to it entitled, *Qurat-al-'Auoon-fi-Tazkira-al-Funun*, narrates the venture of the cultivation of Islamic religious sciences in different parts of Islamic caliphate during eighth and ninth century CE.

A HISTORY OF ISLAMIC LAW

A History of Islamic Law, by N.J. Coulson, published by Edinburgh University Press, paperback edition in 1978, reprint in 1990, traces the history of Islamic law from its formative period up to the modern times. Chapter III — part one, "Jurisprudence in Embryo" and part two, "Islamic Society and Shari'ah Laws" — discusses the course of laws in relation to the social growth. The expansion of the Islamic legal theory, as the author explains has been attributed to its flexible nature that keeps the law and the society intact.

ISLAMIC INSTITUTIONS

The book, *Islamic Institutions*, edited by Muhammad Tahir, published by Anmol Publications, New Delhi, in 1998 contains the following relevant articles:

1. "Some Aspects of Muslim Education and Culture" by Zia-al-Hassan Faruqi.
2. "The Subjects and Titles of Books Written During the First Four Centuries of Islam" by Bayard Doge.
3. "Some Reflections on Islamic Education" by Syed H.H. Nadvi.

The above-mentioned articles have significant relation with

the study of Islamic jurisprudence and other branches of Islamic learning.

CENTRAL ASIA IN THE SIXTEENTH CENTURY

Central Asia in the Sixteenth Century, published by Manohar Publishers, New Delhi, in 2002, is a scholarly work of Mansura Haidar. The esteemed scholar has given a detailed account of the early history of the Uzbeks and Central Asian people in general. It focuses on the socio-political and religious forces that formed a typical identity of Central Asian people in the Islamic history. The work is mainly a detailed study of the events taking into account the factors, which led to the Uzbek occupation of Central Asia.

A CRITICAL STUDY OF THE AL-FARGHANIS TREATMENT OF THE SOURCES IN AL-HIDAYAH

It is my M.Phil. dissertation in Islamic studies. The study was pursued at the Centre of Central Asian Studies (CCAS), The University of Kashmir (2002-04), under the supervision of Prof. G.N. Khaki, Reader, The University of Kashmir. Since this study is a thorough description of the academic venture and the profound scholarship of Central Asian jurists, as such relevant references from this dissertation have also been endorsed.

THE CAMBRIDGE HISTORY OF EARLY INNER ASIA

The Cambridge History of Early Inner Asia, edited by Denis Sinor, published by Cambridge University Press, 1990, reprinted in 1994, introduces the geographical setting of the Central Asian region, the history of different ethnic groups and period-wise breakup of the socio-political occurrences that enabled the nomadic people of Central Asia to perform under the Islamic regime. The chapters, 11 "The Establishment and Dissolution of the Turk Empire" and 13 "The Karakhanids and Early Islam" have special references to the chapters "Socio-Political Milieu" and "Prolific Centres of Islamic Jurisprudence" of the present work.

THE SOCIAL STRUCTURE OF ISLAM

The Social Structure of Islam by Reuben Levy, published by Cambridge University Press, London, UK, in 1957, presents the social institutions of Islam and their evolution in a much systematic manner. It also gives a thorough description of the institutions evolved by Islamic influence in distant regions of the caliphate of Islam. The book provides valuable information of the social structure in the early period of Islam. The esteemed scholar has taken an account of *jahaliya* (ignorance) period, Maccan and Medinan society and traced the gradual development of the social institutions during the Umayyad and the Abbasid periods.

3

Socio-Political Milieu

THE rise and spread of Islam represents one of the most striking events in the history of medieval Central Asia, the territory commonly known in the Islamic chronicles as the Mawara al-Nahr (Transoxiania). The impact of Islam revolutionized the unstable circumstances prevailing in this region during eighth and ninth century CE. When the Sassanid cities were conquered by the Muslims, they got transformed into a staging place for the organized conquest of the entire Transoxiania. The progress of the Muslims in this region took place mainly due to the Islamic organized theme in addition to the internal disputes between the rival tribes and the subsequent internecine strife among the Turks. The impact of Islam on Transoxianian tribal society was so great that it paved the way for the establishment and advancement towards a more sophisticated stage of civilization contributing significantly to the development of social institutions.[1]

Prior to the Muslim conquest of Central Asia in CE 715, the entire structure of society and polity was based on tribal and clan settings. In spite of being martial and striking people, they had transformed this region into a centre of intra-tribal and socio-political activities. To a large extent the people of this region remained nomadic moving here and there in search of

---

[1] H.A.R. Gibb, *The Arab Conquests in Central Asia*, New York, 1970, pp. 96-97.

waters and pastures, and excelled in horsemanship and archery. The social structure represented a typical nomadic people whose livelihood had depended on stock-breeding and hunting. At this stage they had not constructed permanent settlements or cities rather their art and culture had been of a primitive kind devoid of any foreign influence.[2] To a large extent their economy was dominated by certain domestic animals principally the sheep and the horse, but also the ox and the camel. The breeding of these animals involved the use of grass lands, and since it was impossible to use one area indefinitely for this purpose. So these tribes were forced to move from one place to another along with their temporary settlements.[3]

The nomadic tribes of medieval Central Asia preferred sheep and goats over other livestock as they were economically valuable. These animals provided wool out of which tents could be made, their skin could be used as clothing, their dung burnt for warmth, their flesh was eaten and they also yielded milk. Horses were of particular value and played an important role in the military, religious and artistic life of the tribal people.[4]

The womenfolk and children had been extremely engaged with their household. In addition to this they were given the work of knitting tents, preparing cloths, grazing the cattle, preservation of grains and protection of family as they were trained in martial arts and archery. The family structure was based on polygamy and the wives (*khatuns*) of tribal heads were held in great esteem. They sometimes provided valuable suggestions and the tribal heads often respected their opinion while dealing with the matters of tribal design-making.[5]

---

[2] Akbar Ahmad, *Islam in Tribal Societies*, Britain, 1984, p. 221.

[3] Denis Sinor (ed.), *The History of Early Inner Asia*, Britain, 1994, p. 336.

[4] Ibid., pp. 337-38.

[5] Ibid., p. 325.

The nomadic tribes namely Uzbeks, Uighurs, Mongols, Qazaqs, Qirghiz and Turks living around Tashqand, Andijon, Samarkand and Kashgar lived widely in the fields without permanent settlements. Jenkinson holds:

> Every tribal head had his horde or people about them with their wives, children and cattle, who, having consumed the pasture in one place, removed into another and when they move, they have houses like tents set upon a wagon or carts drawn place to place with camels and therein their wives, children and all their riches, which are little, are carried about and every man hath four or five wives. Use of money they have none but barter their cattle for apparel and other necessaries.[6]

Ultimately, there existed no firm political authority that could unite the unruly tribes against any expected external danger. As a result, steppe people lacked political protection especially during eighth century CE. The progress of the Muslims was much halted by internal disputes between the rival tribal factions anxious to snatch or conquer each other's territory, pastures and fields by seditious acts. In fact, all these circumstances prevailing in the region enabled the Muslims to reassert their dominion over the steppe territory.[7]

Lacking political unity and effective leadership, the lands around the Oxus (Jayhun)[8] became the target of the Muslims during the last two decades of seventh century CE. When Khurasan fell into the hands of Muslims, its conquest opened a series of conquests in western Central Asia. These conquests included the lands around the Oxus and those beyond, i.e. Transoxiania. In CE 712, the Arab general Qutaybah bin Muslim

---

[6] Jenkinson, *Hakluyt Society Series*, London, 1997, p. 458.

[7] Mansura Haider, *Central Asia in the Sixteenth Century*, Delhi, 2002, pp. 54-55.

[8] Gibb, op. cit., p. 104.

invaded the adjacent provinces of the Oxus and opened a magnificent chapter of the Muslim conquests that paved the way to transform the history of Transoxania for all times to come.[9]

Before the advent of Islam in this region, the people had been professing the religions like Buddhism, Zoroastrianism and Christianity. The principality of Usrushana (Modern Shakhristan in Uzbek Republic), appears to have been particularly attached to Zoroastrianism which held out there until the middle of ninth century CE.[10]

The reputed and noted historian, Ibn Nadeem states:

> Shamaniya, whose prophet is Buddha, was the religion of the majority of the people of the land beyond the "River" Mawara al-Nahr before Islam.[11]

Buddhism was deeply mixed with Shamanism and social rituals, customs and traditions were professed according to pagan concepts of Zoroastrianism and Buddhism. The staunch believers of Buddhism may have created some resistance in Merv and Samarkand but had probably died out just before the advent of Islam.[12] The believers of Christianity were also found in this region and had received a kind of "Minority" status (*dhimis*) from the caliphate in CE 823, hence professed their Christian beliefs without any disturbance. In addition to these religions, the followers of Manichaeism and Judaism also appear to have been there who constructed monasteries in Merv and Samarkand.[13]

---

[9] Gibb, op. cit., p. 97.

[10] Ibid., p 108.

[11] Ibn Nadeem, *Al-Fihrist,* Cairo, vol. 2, p. 118.

[12] Ibid., p. 113.

[13] Ibid., p. 116.

With the advent of Islam in Central Asia, the socio-political institutions got re-established and a fresh consideration was given to restructure the society according to the Arabo-Islamic tenets. The people now publically affiliated themselves with the new set-up to have an opportunity to participate in the various aspects of the society and the state. In the course of Islamization, Central Asia came to be known as Bilad-al-Islam (the Land of Islam). It not only became the Muslim conquered territory but also a centre of Islamic learning which contributed an immense share to the development of Islamic religious and social sciences. Simultaneously, the series of conquests was going on in the territories of the East onwards by Abdullah bin Talha (CE 830-45) and his son Tahir. Tahir, records Al-Baladhuri:

> He conquered places which had not been reached by any before him.[14]

While conquering the new lands certain socio-legal and administrative issues such as the stable economy, social justice and restoration of the Islamic culture were often faced by the caliphate.[15] As the jurisdiction of the *qazi* (legal authority) extended to Muslims only, the non-Muslim subject population retained their own traditional and tribal institutions.[16]

Socio-Political Scenario During the Umayyad Period

The political organization of the Islamic state under the Umayyad dynasty (AH 41–132/CE 661–750) is recognized as a splendid phase of the Islamic history. Despite some unfortunate events that struck its existence and due to their attempt over the Hashmites, its socio-administrative and strategic plan is still earmarked as one of the best in realm of the dynasty rule in Islam. The entire administrative set-up

---

14 Baladhuri, *Futuh al-Buldhan,* Cairo, 1959, p. 420.

15 Ibid., p. 421.

16 Gibb, op. cit., pp. 94-95.

was build upon the firm design of the executive (*shura*) and judicial functions (*al-qaza*) were carried out in due consultation with the legal experts. The Umayyad rule not only witnessed the political consolidation but their extension towards Central Asia and the adjacent territories is also a hallmark in the Muslim history. The territories of Khurasan fell to the Muslims during CE 663-71 and it was in CE 674 that the Muslims crossed Oxus to annex Bukhara and Eastern Turkistan with the Islamic domain. The Umayyad government, as mentioned in the Muslim chronicles, was based upon the strong administrative offices and institutions which performed various socio-political and administrative functions. The central authority of the government thus comprised of the following segments:

1. The caliph (head of the state)
2. The *shura* (consultative counsel)
3. The *qaza* (judiciary)
4. The *diwan* which included — (a) *diwan al-jund* (military board), (b) *diwan al-kharaj* (the board of finance), (c) *diwan al-rasail* (the board of correspondence), (d) *diwan al-khatam* (the board of signet), and (e) *diwan al-barid* (the board of post).[17]

Besides this administrative set-up, the Umayyad Islamic society was the mixture of various ethnic groups, tribes and identities that include:

1. The feudal aristocracy
2. Military class
3. *Mawalis*
4. *Dhimis*
5. Small landlords

[17] M. Sohail, *Administrative and Cultural History of Islam*, Delhi: Adam Publishers, pp. 64-65.

6. Artisans
7. Slaves
8. Non-Arab elite
9. *'Ulama.*[18]

As per the Islamic concept of the state hierarchy, the caliph represented the supreme political power and his subordinate officials (*wuzara*) possessed judicial competence within the territorial or functional limits of their administrative duties. For the smooth functioning of the administrative set-up in Central Asia, the Umayyad Caliph Walid-I (AH 86-96/CE 705-15) introduced the additional administrative offices which include *'umal* (provincial governors), *muqadamat-al-jaysh* (army commanders), *amin-al-khaza'in* (master of the treasury), *'aamil-al-suq* (market inspector), *al-siqaya* (officials of water supply), *al-shurta* (police) and *qazis* (judges) to ensure an effective and just social mechanism within the territorial limits of the caliphate.[19]

The *qazis*, it is to mention here, were not the law-givers, rather the profound legal authorities sanctioning approvals to resolve the issues of socio-religious importance. Their utmost concern was to look into the legal provisions and procedures and to implement what they could understand suitable (*mustahsan*) within the Shari'ah limits. They used to issue *fatawas* (decrees) as much as they thought suitable to the existing circumastances. While dealing with the socio-religious and economic policies, the *qazi*'s outrightly felt the need of considering the existing circumstances as major challenge to implement the Islamic verdict.[20]

---

[18] M. Sohail, op. cit., p. 67.

[19] E.J. Brill, *Encyclopaedia of Islam*, Leiden, 1953, vol. 2B, pp. 544-45.

[20] M. Khudri, *Tarikh al-Tashrih al-Islami*, Cairo, 1967, p. 97.

The *mufti*'s (jurisconsult) and the *qazi*'s office (*dar-al-ifta*) had become the central organ for the administrative and judicial system. The effective and vibrant judicial mechanism demanded speedy disposal of the issues for which Muslim jurists could play a significant role. Thus the study of Islamic jurisprudence had become imperative throughout the caliphate. The office of the *qazi* has been of prime importance as it served the purpose of implementing the juristic verdicts to the socio-economic and religious requirements. This prestigious office has been recipient of new challenges as well as of emerging trends that could be the result of the social change. Thus, the *mufti*'s and the *qazi*'s had been delegates of the Islamic law, interpreting what has been suitable to best of their understanding. Here it is reported

> The office of *qazi* itself was an Islamic institution typical of the Umayyad period, in which care for elementary administrative efficiency and the tendency to Islamize the society went hand in hand.

It was through the practice of the *qazi*s that the administrative and legal subject matter predominating in the text caught attention of the scholars and studies began to be carried out in search of the possible advance especially in the discipline of Islamic jurisprudence. Not only this, but it proved to be the ripe time for the compilation of Prophetic Sunnah as well as allied knowledge disciplines such as language, logic and philosophy.[21]

By end of the Umayyad regime (AH 132/CE 750), *fuqaha*s (jurists), *mufti*s and *qazi*s advanced much far from their actual position and had now been taken the key position in the politics as well as in the statecraft. These "specialists" were held in great esteem both in the public and administrative circles and could play a vital role to appoint or remove any official of the

[21] Brill, op. cit., p. 548.

state. They owned the authority for single-minded concern that was to formulate the legal structure mandated through the Shari'ah law.[22]

Socio-Political Circumstances During the Abbasid Period

The Abbasids came to power after the downfall of Umayyads in AH 132/CE 750. The polity and society, both, at that time had been entering to a phase of new explanation of a variety of issues and events. The science of Islamic jurisprudence, at this momentum, acquired its essential features and the legal theorists appeared on the scene to interpret the whole corpse of the interpretations into a new dynamism. The formulation of the schools of law in Islam and preparation of the interpretative compendiums are in fact attributed to this era. The early Abbasid rulers continued and reinforced the Islamizing trend to spin both, society and politics, in that direction. The Abbasids patronized the literary tradition and it was in this period that the high-statured scholars and specialists in religious sciences emerged. The jurists, who had been the then legal experts, were recognized as the architects of *Nazm al-khilafah* (the organization of the Islamic caliphate) to redirect towards a just and virtuous society. It was during the Abbasid regime that the Muslim scholars and intellectuals led no stone untouched for the promotion and cultivation of a variety of human and revealed sciences.[23]

The Abbasid caliphs, especially from al-Mansur's reign in CE 755 onwards, extended the domains of the Shari'ah courts throughout the caliphate. In this judicial and extension process, the chief vicinities of medieval Central Asia such as Aspahan, Asbijab, Merghinan, Farghana, Rai, Neshapur, Herat, Bukhara, Khawarizm, Samarkand, Shash and Andijon witnessed a number

---

[22] Brill, op. cit., pp. 549-50.

[23] Ibid., p. 556.

of social and administrative institutions alien to the earlier phase of the Islamic society and polity.[24] These courts, as we are told, organized the legal experts and connected them to the central authority of *Qazi-al-quzah* (the chief judge of the caliphate). In this learned venture, the provincial governors (*'umals*) and judges (*qazis*) had to oblige to the highest legal authority and make him aware of the situations as well as the resolutions they passed. The appointment of the *Qazi-al-quzah*, was done by the caliph and until relieved of his office, he must apply nothing but the sacred law (*ahkam-al-Islam*).[25]

The renowned Abbasid caliph, Harun al-Rashid (AH 170-93/CE 786–809) was very much interested in the expansion of knowledge institutions throughout the caliphate. Among his predecessors, he ranks first to patronize all the available knowledge traditions and invited learned men of different creeds to Baghdad. To get the maximum benefit from Greek, Indian, Chinese and Sassanid thought, he established "Diwan al-Tarajim", a translation bureau to benefit from the eminent works of the world compiled in religious, mathematical and philosophical sciences. This "translation bureau" worked in a literary circle/institution called "Bayt-al-Hikmah" (the House of Wisdom). The scholars and professionals of different sciences, associated with this institution received handsome salaries and caliphal grants on a monthly basis.[26]

Harun al-Rashid, as mentioned above, was a patron of knowledge tradition. He tried utmost to unify and restructure the legal, socio-economic and political institutions throughout his caliphate. The appointment of Imam Abu Yusuf as *Qazi-al-quza* took place for the same reason. Imam Abu Yusuf, an

24 S. Saulat, *Millat-i-Islami ki Mukhtasr Tarikh,* Delhi, 1994, vol. I, p. 226.

25 E.J. Brill, op. cit., p. 556.

26 Saulat, op. cit., p. 193.

outstanding scholar as well as an eminent jurist, had compiled marvellous works in the field of Islamic jurisprudence. Among his renowned treatises include *Kitab-al-Kharaj*, a treatise-cum-*magnum opus* on fiscal and revenue laws of Islam. Abu Yusuf, as the highest legal authority of the Abbasid court, could appoint *qazi*s as well as frame the socio-legal ordinances under the authority of the caliph. The chief *qazi*, Imam Abu Yusuf, has been an eminent disciple of Imam Abu Hanifa, the founder of Hanafi School of Islamic jurisprudence. It was primarily out of the efforts of Imam Abu Yusuf that Hanafi interpretations of the law became familiar to major regions of the caliphate with regard to the socio-religious issues. This verily has been a prolific approach to bring uniformity into the legal theory as well as in its application. The reputed historian, Ibn al-Barr remarks:

> Imam Abu Yusuf's service as *qazi-al-quzah* is the most remarkable appointment in the Abbasid regime.[27]

In addition to this, N.J. Coulson, a contemporary orientalist holds the view that

> Abu Yusuf as chief *qazi* was an eminent practical man who was intimately connected with political circles.[28]

The reputed office of *Qazi-al-quzah*, under the Abbasids proved to be the most vigorous and splended institution. It, at once, expounded and facilitated effective socio-legal framework in the early Islamic society. Under the auspicious authority of *Qazi al-quzah* significant development of legal experiences and professionalism took place. Several socio-legal treatises pertaining to the development of Islamic jurisprudence appeared on the scene. These works supplied huge ideological as well as instrumental stuff for dissemination of Islamic

---

27 Ibn Barr, *Al-Intiqa*, Cairo, AH 1350, p. 172.

28 N.J. Coulson, *A History of Islamic Law*, Cambridge, 1990, p. 51.

knowledge system to centuries to come. The institutions evolved under the authority of *Qazi-al-quzah* ensured speedy disposal of the socio-political issues and this office remained the primary concern of the caliph. The Abbasid rulers divided the entire region of Mawara al-Nahr into several *wilayat*s (provinces) under the authority of governors who supervised these regions in due consultation and assistance by *qazi*s and *mufti*s. The socio-political circumstances, legal issues and administrative affairs of Mawara al-Nahr were brought to the notice of *wazir-al-a'azam* and *qazi-al-quzah*, who would try to resolve the issues in consultation and authority of the caliph.[29]

The major socio-political and administrative institutions which the Abbasids introduced in medieval Central Asia include:

DIWAN-AL-QAZA

The institution of *Diwan-al-qaza* (office of the justice) was among the significant socio-political institutions. It was established to settle and resolve the issues of socio-religious importance. *Qazi* was the supreme religious authority assisted by the legal advisors (*kutub*), jurists (*fuqaha*) and *mufti*s. The office of *qazi* possessed the judicial authority and would demonstrate or interpret any socio-political discourse for the emerging trends in the Islamic society. These trends and newly emerging trends could be justified under the existing or near future conditions resulting from the mass conversion to Islam in medieval Central Asia.[30]

DIWAN AL-MAZALIM

Diwan al-Mazalim (the court of complaints) was introduced to settle the cases and affairs (*ma'amalat*), particularly dealing with

---

[29] Ibn al-Athir, *Al-Kamil fi al-Tarikh*, Beirut, 1977, vol. I, p. 202.

[30] E.J. Brill, op. cit., p. 577.

complaints against the behaviour or the judgements of *qazis* or *'umal*. The in-charge of this office was known as Sahib-al-Mazalim, who held this court in a private building called *diwan* (office). The cases were brought to the notice of *Qazi-al-quzah*, and the caliph himself had to listen to the supreme judicial authority in this office. Very soon formal courts of complaints, "Al-Nazr-fi-al-Mazalim" was set up and their jurisdiction became to a great extent concurrent with that of the *qazi*'s tribunals. By and by this court spread over a vast area of operation much wider than the enquiry into complaints against officials of the state.[31]

DIWAN AL-JARAIM

Diwan al-Jaraim (the court-in-charge of crimes) acted as the tribunals to solve the issues related to crimes and unlawful acts committed by government officers, powerful individuals, influential and authoritative people in the society. The officer-in-charge was called *wali-al-jaraim* assisted by eminent *muftis* to set the cases pertaining to the criminal charges. These courts relied upon the circumstantial evidences, heard the testimony of witness of dubious and doubtful characters, put them on oath and cross-examined them; they imprisoned suspects, convicted on the basis of known character and previous offence; and provided their solution according to the Shari'ah law.[32]

These courts normally respected the substance of Shari'ah and could apply *hadd* or fixed punishment (*tazir*), as per the Shari'ah standards of proof (*al-thabut wa al-bayyinah*).[33]

DIWAN AL-MUHTASIB

Diwan al-Muhtasib was the typical office introduced by the Abbasids. The Abbasid caliphs introduced this institution for

---

[31] Ibn Nadeem, op. cit., p. 213.

[32] Ibid., p. 216.

[33] Ali al-Mawardi, *Kitab al-Ahkam al-Sultaniyah*, Cairo, p. 181.

the general supervision of the religious and moral duties throughout the caliphate including the territories of Central Asia. This *diwan*, as they had practised it in Baghdad, was an essential organ of the social administration. The officer-in-charge was called *muhtasib* whose duties ranged from the enforcement of the Islamic obligations such as *salah* (prayers), *saum* (fast), *zakat* (announcement of legal alms) to the proper segregation of the sexes in the public places, cultivating morals (*aadab*) and good behaviour. *Muhtasib* had the particular authority to deal similarly with petty offences committed in the market places, such as the hoarding of foodstuff or the fraudulent concealment of defects in merchandize (*al-naqais fi al-tijarah*) and investigation into weights and measures (*al-nazar-fil-al-makilat wa al-mazunat*).[34] *Muhtasib* acted in the cases and generally beneath the *qaiz*'s dignity.[35]

With the decline of the Abbasid rule in CE 1258, some powerful dynasties among Muslims had already sprang up and began to rule different parts of the Islamic world. The Samanids (CE 874–1005) ruled Mawara al-Nahr, the Boids (CE 934–1055) ruled Iraq and Eastern Persia and the Fatimids (CE 909–1171) ruled North Africa. With the end of the thirteenth century CE, Islamic society and polity, in these regions, entered a phase of collapse, confronting much serious problems related to law, justice and the administration.[36]

Socio-Political Circumstances During the Rule of Sundry Dynasties

From AH 261/CE 873 onwards, Mawara al-Nahr (Transoxiania) fell to the Samanids who ruled this region up to AH 395/CE 1005. The founder of this dynasty Saman was a convert to Islam during the governorship of Asad bin 'Abdullah al-

[34] Ali al-Mawardi, *Kitab al-Ahkam al-Sultaniyah*, Cairo, p. 187.

[35] Coulson, op. cit., p. 53.

[36] Saulat, op. cit., p. 238.

Qushairi (d. CE 738). His son Asad and four grandsons Nuh, Ahmad, Yahya and Ilyas, who entered the caliphal service and defended the Abbasid caliphate against the Turks around Asbijab. They organized successful expeditions against Mongols and nomads of Shawghar as well. In CE 819, they were granted the governorships of Samarkand (Nuh), Farghana (Ahmad), Shash (Yahya) and Herat (Ilyas). Later on Ahmad's son Nasr became the master of Transoxiania and maintained its vigour for several decades. In CE 875, the Abbasid caliph Mutamid formally confirmed his rule and takeover of Bukhara in the previous year by Nasr's brother Isma'il. In CE 888, Isma'il was given official recognition by the caliphate and ruled from CE 892–907.[37]

The Samanids ruled Mawara al-Nahr from CE 873–1005, with their political and administrative headquarters in Bukhara. The Samanids were the Amirs of Khurasan and Mawara al-Nahr with their capital in Bukhara. The inner core of their state was governed by various lieutenants appointed from among the dynasty.[38]

The frontier zones of the Samanid dominion were under the *muluk-i-atraf* (the border kings/Amirs), who were often from local dynasties. As a consequence, Perso-Islamic legacy set foot into Transoxianian cities and the culture entered a new phase of transition and transformation. With the result, this region became not only a great centre of Arabo-Islamic learning but the birthplace of "New Persian" and the cradle of Perso-Islamic literature.[39]

During the reign of Nasr II (CE 913-42), patronage was given to the Islamic *'ulum*. Nasr was a great patron of literature.

---

[37] Sinor, op. cit., p. 347.

[38] Narakhshi, *Tarikh-i-Bukhara,* tr. R.N. Frye, Cambridge, 1954, p. 84.

[39] Sinor, op. cit., p. 346.

He collected various compilations and manuscripts on different branches of learning, rearranged the material and maintained the libraries. His son Nuh I (CE 942-54) established a grand library in Bukhara which carried the books on history, Quranic sciences, *Hadith* literature, philosophy, medicine, logic and Islamic jurisprudence.[40] Ibn Sina (CE 980–1037), a great scientist and philosopher of Samanid era comments:

> Nuh's library has valuable and extraordinary collections on almost all the arts and sciences.[41]

Ibn Khalikan records:

> Some books are so rare that they were hardly to be traced anywhere else.[42]

The Samanid rulers established *rabats* (border defences) against unruly tribesmen who were a big threat to the Muslim population of the eastern lands. These *rabats* (bourder defences), often busy with men and arms, served the frontiers under the unexpected circumstances. Besides the military expeditions, the Muslim merchants, caravans and settlers penetrated steppe dominions and *sūfīs* (mystics) journeyed to preach and propagate the Islamic faith. The missionary zeal of *'ulama*, scholars and *sūfīs* was encouraged by the Samanid rulers that also resulted in mass conversion to Islam in this region.[43]

One of the noteworthy developments during the Samanid period, as recorded by the contemporary chronicles, is the mass conversion of the local population to Islam. The renowned historians Ibn Miskawiah and Ibn al-Athir report us that in the year CE 960, 200,000 tenants of the Turks went over to Islam.[44]

[40] Saulat, op. cit., pp. 244-45.

[41] Ibid., p. 244.

[42] Ibn Khalikan, *Wafiyat al-Ayan*, Beirut, 1977, vol. IV, p. 137.

[43] Ibid.

[44] Ibid., p. 139.

Reports also tell us that these Turks were the Karakhanids and their tribal followers. Subsequently in the year CE 1043, 10,000 tenants of Turks living between Balasaghun and Balghar accepted Islam.[45] Apart from the patronage of Samanid rulers; Muslim scholars played a significant role to impart Islamic ethical code and education among these tribes. The Muslim scholars tried to reach out to the far-off places of the steppe carrying the mission of Islam which symbolized a fresh political and academic orientation among Islamized Turk tribes.[46]

The Samanid period in Mawara al-Nahr is also earmarked with the credit of patronizing language and literature. During this period, Persian language was officially patronized. In this manner the Arabic and the Persian languages served as the sources of instruction in academic ventures as well as in the official works. The works on law, philosophy, history, mysticism, grammar, medicine and logic were translated into Persian. The famous Persian poet Rudki flourished during the reign of the famous Samanid ruler Nasr II.[47] Moreover *Tarikh-i-Tabari* and *Tafsir-i-Tabari* compiled by the renowned historian Ibn Jarir al-Tabari (AH 224–310/CE 839–923) were translated into Persian. Abu Nasr al-Farabi and Ibn Sina were also associated with the Samanid court. Imam Mansur Maturidi (d. CE 942) and renowned mystic Abu Nasr Sarraj (d. CE 988) also flourished during this time.[48]

The renowned geographers Istakhri, al-Maqdisi and Ibn Hawqal report that the Samanid cities especially Khurasan and Turkistan were the prestigious centres of Islamic learning,

---

[45] Saulat, op. cit., p. 244.

[46] Ibid., p. 245.

[47] Al-Maqdisi, *Ahsan al-Taqasim fi Marifah al-Aqalim*, Cairo, AH 1370, p. 221.

[48] Abu Umar Uthman, *Tabaqat al-Nasiri*, tr. H.G. Raverty, Delhi: Oriental Publishers, vol. I, p. 453.

crafts, fine arts, commerce and agriculture.[49] Samarkand, Bukhara, Merv and Neshapur were famous for literary men, jurisconsults, jurists and *kutubkhanas* which contained grand collections on Islamic religious and social sciences.[50] Al-Maqdisi, in his *magnum opus,* narrates the socio-political scenario of the Samanid period:

> The Samanids are just and virtuous rulers, people respect the law. Knowledge is imparted even to the far-off corners of their domains; people enjoy liberty and social justice. Crimes are not committed openly, the *shurta* (police) is disciplined, the proper network of *madrasas* (schools) adds glamour to the entire region. The scholars and jurists are much venerated. In Khurasan and Mawara al-Nahr people are hospitable, land is fertile, shops and granaries are full of stock. Samarkand is a glorious city famous for the manufacturing of paper; it is also a great centre of learning. Neshapur is the cradle of learning; scholars from far-off places visit its libraries. Balkh is really a paradise of Khurasan. Rai is famous for cleanliness and beauty. Bukhara is known as Qubat-al-Islam, scholars of every discipline serve here; even the common people know the Islamic laws of inheritance and socio-economic aspects of Quran and Sunnah. Islamic jurisprudence is the special concern of *'ulama.* Amirs know their dealings, *muhtasibs* share responsibility, *khatibis* propagate Quran and Sunnah, Khawarizm, Herat and Merv are among the prestigious and prosperous cities of the Samanids.[51]

The Samanids ruled major domains of the Mawara al-Nahr from AH 261–395/CE 874–1005 and during this period the below-mentioned rulers were enthroned: Nasr I (874-92), Isma'il

[49] Abu Umar Uthman, *Tabaqat al-Nasiri,* tr. H.G. Raverty, Delhi: Oriental Publishers, vol. I, p. 588.

[50] Ibid., p. 589.

[51] Akbar Shah Khan Najibabadi, *Tarikh-i-Islam,* Delhi, 1987, vol. III, p. 318.

(892–907), Ahmad (907-13), Nasr II (913-42), Nuh I (942-54), 'Abdul-al-Malik (954-61), Mansur I (961-76), Nuh II (976-97), Mansur II (997-99), 'Abdul-al-Malik (999–1005).[52]

The interior breakdown of the administration and insufficient means to curb the crises on the frontiers were the main causes for the downfall of the Samanids. When the Samanid rule began to collapse, the local dynasties like the Ilkhanids (AH 380–609) and the Karakhanids began to expand towards the Samanid holdings. The Samanids had come to rely increasingly on *ghulam* (slave) armies constituted by the local tribesmen. With the result they controlled the key positions in military and administrative posts. In Khurasan and Ghaznah, Subuktigin (AH 366-87/CE 976-97) established an independent dominion. From CE 1000 onwards, the Samanid dominion was reduced mostly to the areas around Bukhara and Samarkand. In CE 1005, the ruler of Kashgar, Ilk Khan captured Bukhara and Samarkand, resulting in the ultimate end of the Samanid rule in Central Asia. The local dynasties of Mawara al-Nahr like the Karakhanids, the Ilkhanids and the Saljuk Turks achieved respectability within the Islamic orbit and became the masters of this region for the coming centuries.[53]

During reign of the Caliphal-granted authority, dynasties like Samanids, Karakhanids, Ilkhanids and Turks, the entire region of Mawara al-Nahr remained the cradle of Islamic sciences and produced renowned figures in various branches of learning. It seems worthy to mention here that the political disturbances did not affect the academic and socio-religious developments; rather the process of Islamization went on simultaneously along with the severe political atmosphere. These local dynasties as the *'ulama* reasoned "were also orthodox

[52] Akbar Shah Khan Najibabadi, *Tarikh-i-Islam,* Delhi, 1987, vol. III, p. 320.

[53] Saulat, op. cit., p. 268.

Muslims and hence, if that were God's will, were also worthy of rule".[54]

Apart from this situation, when the Ghaznavid empire (AH 366–582/CE 976-1156) weakened, the Seljuk Turks came to throne. Tagrul (AH 429-55), in the battle of Dandaniqan in AH 429/CE 1037 defeated the Ghaznavid ruler Mas'ud (CE 1030-40) and laid the foundation of the Seljuk dynasty in Khurasan.[55] The Seljuk Turks ruled Mawara al-Nahr from AH 429–552/CE 1037–1157 adding academic, artistic and architectural glamour to the famous cities of Rai, Merv and Aspahan in addition to their political domains. The famous Persian poets like M'uizi, Anwari, Nizami (d. CE 1202) and Khaqani (d. CE 1185) enriched the Persian language with best of their poetic versions. Among the renowned theologians, poets and philosophers of this era, we can mention Ghazali (d. AH 505/CE 1111), 'Abdul Qadir Geelani (d. AH 561/CE 1166), 'Umar Khayam (d. AH 526/CE 1132), Jalal-u-din Rumi (d. AH 672/CE 1272), Zamakhshari (d. AH 538/CE 1144), the compiler of *al-Kashaf* a noted exegesis of Quran, Shahristani (d. AH 548/CE 1153), who compiled *al-Milal-wa-Nihal*, Khazani who compiled *Mizan-al-Hikmah*,[56] Hariri (d. AH 516/CE 1122), the compiler of *Muqamat-al-Hariri* and 'Abdullah Ansari (AH 481/CE 1088), a famous *sūfī* who compiled *Risalat-al-Manajat*. Nizam al-Mulk Tusi was the grand *wazir* of Seljuk's who joined the Seljuk service about AH 400/CE 1048. He was well versed in Islamic jurisprudence and Hadith literature. He compiled *Dustur-al-Wuzara* and *Siyasat Namah*, two monumental and reputed works in the field of political science. Nizam al-Mulk is also credited with patronizing the cause of knowledge and founding educational institutions (*madrasas*) into the Muslim domains. He acted as the Sultan's

54 Uthman, op. cit., p. 590.

55 Taj din Subki, *Tabaqat al-Shafiya al-Kubra*, Cairo, vol. III, p. 117.

56 P.K. Hitti, *History of the Arabs*, London, 1970, p. 709.

chief advisor and had a special authority to bring and set together educational, social and religious reforms. The reputed scholar, Taj-u-din Subki describes him as one of the greatest reformers and personalities in the world of Islam.[57]

After the death of Saljuk Sultan Sanjar (d. CE 1157), Atsaz Khawarizmi laid the foundation of an independent domain in Central Asia, known as Khawarizm Shahi sultanate. Sultan 'Alauddin Taksh (AH 568-96) and Muhammad Khawarizm Shah (AH 596–617) proved to be able rulers from this dynasty. Muhammad Khawarizm Shah conquered Mawara al-Nahr and tried to capture Baghdad but Genghis Khan's invasion (CE 1206-27) towards Khawarizm Shahi sultanate overshadowed all the possibilities of advancement towards the East. The Mongol tribal leader Genghis Khan plundered city after city and devastated Khawarizm Shah's sultanate. Muhammad Khawarizm Shah fled to Aabskun and died there in CE 1220.[58]

Jalal-u-din Shah (CE 1220-31), the successor of Muhammad Khawarizm Shah, showed some resistance but Mongol army led by Genghis Khan, destroyed Samarkand, Bukhara, Khawarizm, Balkh, Neshapur and Rai. The unruly tribesmen destroyed mosques, educational institutions and grand libraries full of knowledge and intellectualism. Reports tell us that at least 2,000,000 people perished in Mawara al-Nahr during this invasion in CE 1220. Again in CE 1258, Genghis Khan's grandson Halagu marched with the same purpose, penetrated the boundaries of Mawara al-Nahr doing much more than his grandfather. Halagu destroyed the city of Baghdad, razed it to the ground, ordered mass assassination and destruction of all renowned structures of Islamic civilization.[59]

[57] Saulat, op. cit., p. 366.

[58] Uthman, op. cit., p. 518.

[59] Ibid., p. 522.

The plunder of Mawara al-Nahr by Mongols in the year CE 1258, suspended life for many years and hampered the scholarly and intellectual activities for decades together. Mongols killed 160,000 Muslims in Central Asia and Baghdad during this attack. Grand mosques, hospitals, academic institutions and highest seats of learning were destroyed. As a result, the Muslims living there had to face gigantic challenges associated with their rehabilitation and recovery.[60]

Ultimately, in the year CE 1258, a significant and comprehensive period of the Islamic civilization came to an end. Up to this period, Muslims contributed and controlled almost all the fields of knowledge, statesmanship and prosperity. Honestly speaking, they had no parallel or similar in the world so far. Unfortunately with the Mongol invasion, Muslims were pushed back to far-off distances. Their socio-cultural and political advances were the result of extreme enthusiasm which tied them together to perform to its best till this stage of the world history.[61]

---

[60] Uthman, op. cit., p. 523.

[61] Al-Maqdisi, op. cit., p. 224.

4

Central Asian Jurists
Contribution and Impact

THE Central Asian Muslim jurists have an undisputed share in the realm of Islamic jurisprudence as well as in the contribution to the Islamic legal theory. With the annexation of Mawara al-Nahr to the Islamic caliphate in CE 712, the Muslims of this region enriched Islamic civilization with all the possible and attainable efforts both on academic and administrative fronts. The overall intellectual capacities and human resources were brought to action in order to harmonize the socio-political activities according to the tenets of Islam. The Islamic value system was adopted and efforts for the cultivation of the Islamic sciences began to flourish in major vicinities of this region. From CE 732 onwards, the learned figures of Central Asia began to demonstrate a much distinguished scholarship in almost all the disciplines of Islamic knowledge system. Their enthusiasm and concrete approach expanded the canvas of Islamic sciences to accommodate reliable human experiences into a systematic legal theory to suit the exigent circumstances. In this literary venture, both *'ulama* (scholars) as well as *khulafa* (caliphs) worked hand in hand for the promotion of the Islamic value system as well as for the development of various sciences.[1]

---

[1] Haji Khalifah, *Kashf al-Zunun*, Istanbul, 1941, vol. III, p. 218.

With regard to the study of *fiqh* (Islamic jurisprudence) in Central Asia, one must understand that among the Sunni schools of law, the Iraqi School of Law (Hanafi) proved to be much effective and everlasting in this region. Historically speaking, this particular school of law formed the basis for consolidation of the legal tradition carrying the selective principles, techniques, skills and methods of deducing rulings from a variety of the sources of law. As a result of this process, Mawara al-Nahr got recognition as a great centre of Islamic learning throughout the entire lands of Muslim caliphate. This knowledge tradition attracted the literary and intellectual class across the Muslim lands to inherit from this valuable venture. The Abbasid rulers (CE 750–1258) and the local dynasties patronized the literay tradition and established reputed scholars at central positions of their domains to promote and facilitate the higher standards of academic excellence.[2]

The contemporary sources, compiled in this regard, tell us that the scholars and students even from the distant and far-off lands of North Africa, Arab and Syria gathered here to associate themselves with reputed scholars of various branches of learning. The centres established at Samarkand, Bukhara, Tashqand, Tirmiz, Merv, Kashan, Balkh, Khokand, Farghana, Osh and Marghinan played a significant role to disseminate Islamic knowledge tradition and to acquaint the learners with intellectual and scholarly pursuits.[3]

In the discourse of Islamic jurisprudence, the doctrinal techniques and legal aid rooted in the *fiqh* methodology of the Hanafi School of Law got an opportunity to play its role for the socio-religious demonstration. This demonstration worked for the possibility of resolving issues as per the Islamic value system.

---

[2] M. Tahir, *Islamic Institutions*, Delhi, 1987, p. 418.

[3] S. Saulat, *Milit-i-Islamiyah ki Mukhtasar Tarikh*, Delhi, 1994, vol. III, p. 172.

The valuable legal aid along all its possible cannotations was carried out to Central Asian lands by the prominent and towering jurists like Abu-Mufti Balkhi (d. AH 216), Muhammad bin Shuj'a Balkhi (d. AH 266), Ja'far Balkhi (d. AH 482) 'Alu'udin Muhammad bin Ahmad al-Samarqandi (d. AH 361) and Abu Laith Samarqandi (d. AH 383).[4]

The jurists mentioned above are among the prime architects associated with the development of Islamic jurisprudence in medieval Central Asia. Their socio-religious importance lies with the fact that they transmitted the basic techniques of the legal science and made it available to the coming generations. Among the jurists mentioned, the grand jurist Abu Laith Samarqandi is of great significance. His works, interpretation and understanding of Islamic jurisprudence have been utilized by the towering jurists as reference. In addition to this, his approach as a jurist remained an incredible trend for next two centuries in deducing law from the alternate sources.[5]

While mentioning the contribution to Islamic jurisprudence, the jurists, Ahmad bin Muhammad Shahi al-Samarqandi (d. AH 325), Abu al-Barakat 'Abdullah bin Ahmad al-Nasafi (b. AH 618), Hisam al-din Muhammad Akhsikasi (d. AH 644), Najm al-din Abu Hafas 'Umar bin Muhammad (d. AH 537), Fakhr al-Islam 'Ali bin Muhammad al-Bazudi (d. AH 482), Sa'ad din Mas'ud bin 'Umar Taftazani (b. AH 722), Razi al-din Muhammad al-Saghani (b. AH 577) and 'Ali bin Abu Bakr Marghinani (d. AH 593) have also played an incredible role in the promotion of the Islamic sciences in Central Asia. Taj-u-din Subki, a reputed scholar and historian credits them with consolidating the overall structure of Islamic jurisprudence in Mawara al-Nahr.[6]

---

[4] *Ma'arif*, Delhi, 1984, vol. 134, pp. 352-53.

[5] Ibid., p. 354.

[6] Taj-ud-Din Subki, *Tabaqat al-Shafiyah al-Kubra*, Cairo, vol. III, p. 117.

The jurists, whose contribution and role will be acknowledged in this chapter, are the prime architects regarding the formulation of juristic approaches in this region. The biographical evidences of the contemporary era manifest and ascertain that their highly intellectual and socio-legal understanding could unite and maintain the distinction and peculiarity among all the schools of Islamic law.[7]

Abu Laith Samarqandi

The grand jurist and towering scholar Abu Laith Nasr bin Muhammad bin Ahmad (d. AH 383) generally known as "Imam al-Huda"[8] (the Leader of Righteousness) was a native of Samarkand. He mastered different branches of Islamic learning that include *tafsir, hadith, fiqh, mantiq, falsafah, sirah, tarikh* and *usul al-fiqh* with profound scholarship. Abu Laith is not to be confused with his contemporary scholar Nasr bin Muhammad al-Hafiz al-Samarqandi, as the famous biographer of the jurists, 'Abd al-Qadir al-Qarshi (d. AH 775) did. He, surmisely has committed an error by attributing to the later some of the magnificent works of Abu Laith Samarqandi.[9] 'Abd al-Qadir al-Qarshi, as I think, committed this error due to resemblance of the surname and also by considering their same appellation.[10]

Abu Laith Samarqandi acquired his knowledge by travelling to distant areas of Mawara al-Nahr, Iraq, Arabia and Syria and associated himself with the renowned scholars and jurists. He lived there for months together and excelled in almost all the branches of Islamic sciences. Abu Laith, finally chose to opt for Islamic jurisprudence as he loved to enjoy from the legal debates and discussions. This approach helped

[7] Narakhshi, *Tarikh-i-Bukhara*, tr. Frye, Cambridge, 1954, p. 101.

[8] *Ma'arif*, op. cit., vol. 134, p. 355.

[9] *Dairat al-Ma'arif*, Lahore, Pakistan, 1984, vol. I, p. 104.

[10] Ibid., p. 905.

him in searching for new possibilities as well as to discover all the possible interpretations of the law. Ibn Khalikan, in his *magnum opus*, *Wafiyyat al-A'yan* remarks:

> He gained the confidence of his teachers and became a distinguished figure among his contemporaries which include Abu Bakr Shahuya (d. AH 361), Qazi al-Haramain (d. AH 351), Ahmad bin 'Ali al-Razi (d. AH 370), Abu Bakr Khawarizmi (d. AH 403), Abu-Mansur Maturidi, Muhammad al-Mawarzi (d. AH 344), Hakim Samarqandi (d. AH 342), al-Hindwani (d. AH 362), Ibn al-Tabari, Abu-Bakr Jurjani (d. AH 352), and Abu al-Haitham Qazi al-Neshapuri.[11]

Abu Laith Samarqandi surpassed his teachers and while discussing any legal discourse he would interpret a verdict also in confirmation with *urf* (tradition) of a particular region. This approach made his unique identification in the scholarly circles in Central Asia and Persia. He remained in Samarkand till his last breath and his demise took place in AH 383. His death, as mentioned in the contemporary chronicles, made the scholars and learners restless as they had lost an unparalleled jurist once for ever.[12]

CONTRIBUTION

The grand jurist, approached various branches of Islamic learning and a critical survey of his academic career, would depict that Abu Laith Samarqandi distinguished himself by adopting a much balanced approach while interpreting Islamic legal discourse. He approached various branches of Islamic learning and discovered himself to be fit for the study of Islamic jurisprudence. This was the only attempt as well as an effective relationship that could make a possible union between society and the religion. This reality, as an approach has been

---

[11] *The Cambridge History of Iran*, Cambridge, 1954, vol. IV, p. 476.

[12] Haji Khalifah, *Kashf al-Zunun*, Istanbul, 1941, vol. II, p. 381.

produced in his works in an explored from. Abu Laith Samarqandi, while approaching Quran produced a valuable commentary *al-Tashrih* which was published from Cairo, Egypt in AH 1310. The great scholar Ibn al-Arab (d. AH 854) translated this exegesis into Turkish, Abu al-Fazl Musa al-Azniqi, a contemporary of Ibn al-Arab, added some introductory notes entitled "Anfas al-Jawahir" to enrich this treatise with much advanced legal and intellectual debates.[13]

Among his other famous treatises, the following are mentioned with a brief description to make a thorough study of his authority over various disciplines of Islamic sciences.

Khazanah al-Fiqh

The treatise *Khanazah al-Fiqh* is the famous work compiled in the *fiqh* literature. The esteemed jurist, in this work, discusses and deals with the legal terminology adopted in Islamic jurisprudence. In the same way, narrations from the local usages, customs and social experiences that need the legal sanction. The manuscript of this scholarly treatise was preserved by the Ottoman rulers of Turkey (CE 1299–1451) and the same got translated and published from Istanbul in Turkish language.[14]

Mukhtarat al-Riwayat

The grand jurist, Abu Laith Samarqandi approached some of the significant legal narratations/discourses and pointed out towards the possible deductions that may expand the canvas of Islamic jurisprudence. He observed the nature of certain methods deployed to serve as the alternate sources of the Islamic legal theory. He approached the principles of analogy especially (*qiyas*) and juristic preference (*tarjih*) to legalize the deductions rooted in the social aspect of the religious

[13] *Dairat al-Ma'arif*, Lahore, Pakistan, 1984, vol. I, p. 904.

[14] Ibid., p. 905.

commandments. This treatise is a valuable study of narrations (*riwayat*) to investigate into the nature and scope of the Islamic legal discourse.[15]

Al-Muqadimah fi al-Salat

This particular treatise by Abu Laith Samarqandi covers the significance and benefits of obligatory prayers (*salat al-farz*). The reputed scholar has shown a great concern to look into the juristic differences in order to show the nature of jurictic interpretations particularly in prayers. Later on, commentaries to this treatise appeared in Turkish and Persian languages.[16]

Tanbih al-Gafilin

This reputed work of Abu Laith Samarqandi is an account of the moral and ethical message of Islamic practices. In this treatise special emphasis is laid for the attainment of the moral and ethical perfection in order to establish a secure and responsible society. He narrates different incidents of the companions of the Prophet (SAW) and their followers to focus on the benefit of Islamic practices.[17]

Bustan al-'Aarifin

This work has been authored to highlight the spiritual aspect of Islam. It also provides moral and ethical message to achieve perfection in the religious deeds.[18]

Al-'Aqidah

In addition to the science of Islamic jurisprudence, Abu Laith Samarqandi approached philosophy and logic as well. To defend Islamic beliefs against Greek philosophy and

---

15 P.K. Hitti, *History of the Arabs*, London, Macmillan, 1970, p. 709.

16 *Dairat al-Ma'arif*, op. cit., vol. I, p. 908.

17 Ibid., p. 358.

18 Ibid., p. 359.

rationalism he compiled *Al-'Aqidah* in form of a dialogue. The objective being to introduce the real message of the Islamic belief system and its adequate potential. This reputed work was published by A.W.T. Juynboll in CE 1881 from Germany. Muhammad bin 'Umar al-Navavi (d. AH 1305) wrote its commentary entitled, *Qatr al-Ghays*. The famous orientalist, Joseph Schacht holds that the works of Abu Laith Samarqandi represent him both as a jurist as well as the philosopher for defence of legal and philosophical aspect of Islam.[19]

Ahmad bin Muhammad Shashi al-Samarqandi

Ahmad bin Muhammad Shahi al-Samarqandi (d. AH 325) was also one of the reputed jurists and towering intellectuals of Mawara al-Nahr (Transoxiania) who contributed significantly Islamic jurisprudence. He was born in Shash, a famous village in medieval Central Asia, in about AH 226 and was held with great esteem and honour both by the rulers as well as people. He enriched himself by approaching the different branches of Islamic sciences, made a valuable contribution to the field of Islamic jurisprudence and appeared as a renowned jurist in the Hanafi School of Law. Al-Shashi has been much influenced by the legal techniques and instruments deployed by the Hanafi jurists for deduction of law. The Hanafi legal methodology, as al-Shashi believed, was more reliable and instrumental for the legal deductions. It is, as he asserts, much comprehensive as well as delicate but at the same time based upon the social reality. Besides Quran and Sunnah, it treats several social and human experiences as the notions to be considered in the formulation of legal code. The Hanafi legal methodology, he considered much effective to suit the situations in Central Asia. It was the social plan in Hanafi legal code, he believes, that made it capable of confronting

[19] S. Sulayman Nadvi, *Islam Aur Mustashriqin*, Ma'arif, Delhi, 1985, vol. 135, p. 26.

situations in Central Asia and Iraq. With the emergence of systematic juristic trends in Islamic jurisprudence, he could realize the significance of attaining all the available information in Islamic sciences especially mastering the knowledge of '*usul al-tarjih*' (principles of preferring legal narrations), a delicate and comprehensive field in Islamic jurisprudence. Al-Shashi, while commenting on this subject advocated for the consideration of all such social experiences that expand the scope for the study of social phenomenon. Being an original thinker in the field of socio-legal study, he surpassed many of his contemporaries which include Ibrahim al-Mawarzi (d. AH 330), Abu-Bakr Farsi (d. AH 350), Abu Bakr Saryafi (d. AH 330), Al-Qafal al-Shashi (d. AH 336) and Ibn Haykawyah (d. AH 318).[20]

Ahmad bin Muhammad Shahi al-Samarqandi's doctrinal techniques and juristic expediences have a great impact upon scholars of Central Asia and Iraq which were carried out by the reputed jurists like 'Ala-uddin Samarqandi (d. AH 361) and 'Abd al-'Aziz bin 'Abd al-Rahman Marghinani (d. AH 477). This extensive contribution has marked a new chapter in the study of *hadith* and *fiqh* literature and still believed to be a valuable addition in the field of various Islamic sciences. The scholars who benefited from al-Shashi's methodology of the selective principles (*al-Usul al-Fiqh*) include 'Abd al-Rehman Marghinani's son, Abu al-Hassan Zahirudin (d. AH 506) and his son Hassan bin 'Ali (d. AH 567) the compiler of the books *al-Ahdiya, al-Fatawa, al-Fawa'id* and *al-Shurut*.[21]

CONTRIBUTION

The reputed scholar and jurist, Ahmad bin Muhammad Shashi al-Samarqandi has to this credit some of the valuable compilations that enhanced the scope of the legal theory and equipped it with a systematic pattern. Among his famous

[20] *Encyclopaedia of Islam*, ed. E.J. Brill, Leiden, 1953, vol. IV, p. 558.

[21] Ibid., p. 559.

treatises in the field of Islamic jurisprudence and especially in the field of *Usul al-Fiqh* the following are mentioned.[22]

Usul al-Shashi

This treatise is considered to be the most critical work on *usul al-fiqh* (fundamentals of Islamic jurisprudence). The book is still within the curricula of religious seminaries in Iraq, Central Asia and Indo–Pak subcontinent. Moreover, it has also remained in the syllabi of Nizamiyyah and Mustansiriyyah institutions founded by Nizam al-Mulk Tusi and the Abbasid caliph Mustansir Billah during the epoch of tenth century CE. Its Egyptian edition appeared around AH 1189. Haji Khalifa, a reputed biographer as well as historian has mentioned and referred to this valuable treatise by the title *Kitab al-Khamees*.[23]

Tarikh Jami al-Kabir

The works of Imam Muhammad al-Shaybani (d. AH 189) forms the basis of Hanafi School of Law. These works as discussed in the earlier chapter carry the distinguished legal concepts and instruments mentioned in the Hanafi legal methodology. Among these treatises is his reputed work *Jami al-Kabir*, which was successfully annotated by al-Shashi. Later on, its commentary was written by Hassan al-Farabi by the title *Fusul al-Hawashi*. This reputed commentary was published as an epilogue to *Usul al-Shashi* to highlight its juristic distinction and legal significance. The commentary has also been published as a separate treatise by Egyptian publishers.[24]

Among the Indian commentators on *Usul al-Shashi*, we may mention Barkatullah Muhammad Lakhnavi's commentary *Ahsan al-Hawashi* and Faiz al-Hassan Gangohi's *Umdat al-Hawashi*.[25]

[22] Gangohi, *Zafr al-Muhasilin*, Deoband, 1996, p. 280.

[23] Haji Khalifah, op. cit., vol. IV, p. 1632.

[24] Gangohi, op. cit., p. 282.

[25] Ibid.

These commentaries for the first time in Indian subcontinent elaborated some of the significant aspects of legal methods deployed in al-Shashi's system.

Ahmad bin Muhammad Shashi, throughout his scholarly carrier lived a simple and mystic life and never tried to visit nobles or the ruling class. In fact, he never liked any sort of publicity or pretention. Consequently, our sources to enter his realm of scholarship are limited. Even the popular Muslim biographers remain silent regarding his academic career. As a result no exact record of his treatises has been kept by the contemporary biographers and narrators. While discussing a particular legal issue, al-Shashi approaches to the interpretations from various schools of law and finally discusses the legality of the Hanafi viewpoint through reliable, balanced and systematic approach.[26]

Ahmad bin Muhammad al-Shashi passed away in Egypt in AH 325 and left behind him some rare manuscripts which have been preserved in Khudevia Museum, Egypt.[27]

Abu al-Barakat 'Abdullah bin Ahmad al-Nasafi

The reputed scholar and jurist Abu al-Barakat 'Abdullah bin Ahmad is among the distinguished and renowned scholars of Central Asia who contributed a lot to the development of Islamic sciences. He was born in Nasf in AH 618. This region has been famous for the scholars circles throughout the Islamic caliphate. His native town Nasf, as reported by Ibn Khalikan, had already produced some noted figures in various branches of Islamic sciences. Abu al-Barakat 'Abdullah bin Ahmad, since his childhood, was very much interested in scholarly persuits and knowledge discussions. He acquired his knowledge by travelling to reputed centres and scholars available at that

---

[26] Ahmad bin Muhammad, *Usul al-Shashi*, Beirut, 1982, pp. 6-7.

[27] Gangohi, op. cit., p. 283.

time. During the course of his study he associated himself with the noted jurists who flourished in Mawara al-Nahr enabling him to discover the utmost trends and dimensions in the field of Islamic jurisprudence. Soon after the studying and examining the *masmu'at* (legal reports) and *marwiyat* (narratives) of the various schools of law, al-Nasafi realized the significance of this field and chose it for his entire scholarly career. After a brief survey into the legal deductions of various schools of law, he approached the Hanafi legal methodology and thought it much rational as well as adaptable. It was the ultimate concern of the Hanafi jurists, realized, al-Nasafi, that this system covered social phenomenon much effectively and had the capacity to reconcile between text and the society. To him, it was a big chellenge for the jurists to formulate the legal discourse by considering the larger interest of the society. Being a keen observer of the social happenings, al-Nasafi tried to explain the religious verdicts within the social context. He mastered various branches of Islamic sciences (*ulum*) and approached almost all the disciplines of knowledge available during his time. As per the arrangement and agreement of the jurists within the Hanafi School, he ranks in the *al-tabqat al-sittah* (sixth category) of the jurists, whose expertise lies in distinguishing the ordinary, sound, balanced and appropriate interpretation for the formulation of the legal precept. Moreover, this category of the experts has been associated with analysing a variety of legal deductions to formulate a discourse to suit the circumstances:

و الطبقة السادسة من فقهاء الأحناف أصحاب الصحيح و التمييز كابى البركات عبد الله بن
احمد صاحب كنز الدقائق و در المختار و الوقاية .

And sixth category of the Hanafi jurists is 'Ashab al-Tamiz wa al-Sahih' which comprises of the jurists like 'Abdullah bin Ahmad Nasafi, the author of *Kanz al-Daqaiq*,

Dur al-Mukhtar and *al-Wiqayah*.[28]

During the course of his academic career, he spent four years in Bukhara and Samarkand to elevate his scholarship as well as to get maximum benefit out of the scholarly experiences available here. He approached the renowned treatises in the field of Islamic jurisprudence authored by the Muslim jurists from time to time. It is in Samarkand, that he was influenced by the distinguished jurists like Shamas al-Aima 'Abd al-Satar Kardari, Hamid bin Zarir and Imam Badr al-din Khawarzadah who had been the monumental figures in the field of Islamic jurisprudence. It is undoubtly the association with these scholars that al-Nasafi could gain benefit and expertise in formulating the legal interpretations as per the demanding circumstances. The scholars mentioned above have been considered as the masters of analogical deduction in absence of a clear textual commandment.[29] Al-Qarshi, one of the noted biographers in the Muslim history, holds the view that al-Nasafi, mastered *fiqh* from Kardari, narrated Shayybani's *Ziyadat* from Ahmad bin 'Atabi, and *Usul al-Fiqh* from 'Allama Saqnaqi of Neshapur, the scholars known for their intellect as well as for virtuous life in the entire region, the scholars held with great esteem by the natives of Neshapur, Bukhara and the adjacent provinces.[30]

Al-Nasafi, after living a passionate scholarly life, died in AH 710 in Ajez, a vicinity of Neshapur, leaving behind him a number of magnificent works in the field of Islamic jurisprudence and other Islamic sciences which were transmitted to the coming generations by his eminent disciples.[31]

---

[28] Qasim Shah Bukhari, *Maqalat al-Nabigah*, Delhi, 1999, p. 9.

[29] Gangohi, op. cit., p. 267.

[30] Al-Qarshi, *Jawahar al-Muziah*, Cairo, 1896, vol. I, p. 188.

[31] Haji Khalifah, op. cit., vol. III, p. 283.

CONTRIBUTION

Al-Nasafi compiled most of his works in the field of Islamic jurisprudence that include *Matan al-Wafi, Kafi, al-Manar fi-Ilm al-Usul, Kashf al-Asrar, Mussafi, al-'Atimad, Madarik al-Tanzil* and *Kanz al-Daqaiq*.[32]

Among the works mentioned above, *Kanz al-Daqaiq* is considered to be the most critical as well as much complicated treatise ever authored in the field of Islamic jurisprudence.

Kanz al-Daqaiq and Its Commentaries (Shurah)

The monumental work, *Kanz al-Daqaiq* is among the basic works compiled in Hanafi *fiqh* literature. This noted work, exclusively deals with the resolution of the socio-religious, political and economical issues confronted by the Muslims. The jurists of the other schools of law consider it to be an authoritative work for understanding the systematic legal discourse and its explanation especially in context of the scholarly persuits in Iraq and Mawara al-Nahr. The narrations in the book have been in consonance with the Shayabani's *Zahir al-Riwayah* annotated and elaborated by various Hanafi jurists to set a sound and balanced legal discourse. Besides this, the references and discourses from the grand jurists like Abu Hanifa, Abu Yusuf and Zufr bin Hazil have also been manifested. This renowned scheme has added to the glamour of this reputed work and made it a *magnum opus* to understand the Hanafi doctrinal methodology.[33]

على الكنز فى الفقه الشروح كثيرة　　بحار تفيد الطالبين لإلياء

و لكن بهذا البحر صارت صواقيا　　و من ورد البحر إستقل سواقيا

[32] Ibn Najim, *Bahr al-Raiq*, Delhi, 1932, vol. II, p. 222.

[33] Haji Khalifah, op. cit., vol. III, p. 107.

The commentaries upon this monumental treatise include the following:

Al-Bahr al-Raiq fi Sharah-i-Kanz al-Daqaiq

This commentary was written by the renowned jurist Zain al-'Aabidin bin Ibrahim commonly known as Ibn Najim (d. AH 970). He annotated up to *Kitab al-Ijarah* and unfortunately with his death, the task of elaborating the juristic themes remained incomplete till the arrival of Muhammad bin Hassan al-Shaheer (d. AH 991) who carried the work with utmost zeal and completed it. The book has also been annotated by many other scholars of Mawara al-Nahr, Egypt and Syria along the compulsory notes.[34]

Tab'in al-Haqaiq

This commentary on *Kanz al-Daqaiq* was compiled by Fakhrudin Abu-Muhammad 'Uthman (d. AH 743).[35]

Sharah Kanz al-Daqaiq

This commentary was written by Moin-ud-din Haravi who mastered the legal techniques of *tarjih* (knowledge of the juristic preference) in the Hanafi methodology.[36]

Ramz al-Haqaiq

This commentary was compiled by Qazi-Badruddin Muhammad bin Ahmad (d. AH 855). The reputed commentator has minutely looked into the various aspects of the social changes as well as to the emerging legal trends resulting due to the socio-cultural interaction and needs a thorough study and insight.[37]

---

[34] *Encyclopaedia of Islam*, vol. IV, p. 507.

[35] Haji Khalifah, op. cit., vol. II, p. 1008.

[36] Ibid., vol. III, p. 1009.

[37] Gangohi, op. cit., p. 269.

Al-Mulaqab al-Faqih

It was written by Muhammad bin 'Abd al-Rehman al-'A'ini (d. AH 882).[38]

Al-Nahr al-Faiq

This commentary was written by Ibrahim bin Muhammad (d. AH 1105).[39]

Al-Fara'id fi-Hal al-Musail wa al-Qawa'id

This commentary is considered to be an exemplary work on al-Nasafi's *Kanz al-Daqaiq*. It was written by Mustafa bin Boli (d. AH 915). The special feature of this commentary is its elucidative approach to unveil the hidden and complicated interpretations of the text. The reputed scholar insists to comprehend all the possible deductions and approaches the text through the Hanafi point of view.[40]

Mustakhlas al-Haqaiq

This commentary was written by Sheikh Ibrahim bin Muhammad Qari (d. AH 970).[41]

Fath al-Masalik

This commentary was written by 'Abd al-Rahman 'Isa al-'Umari (d. AH 1157).[42]

Sharah

It is a noteworthy commentary on *Kanz al-Daqaiq* by Qutub din Muhammad bin Muhammad (d. AH 950).[43]

---

[38] Gangohi, op. cit., p. 269.

[39] Ibid., p. 262.

[40] Ibid., p. 270.

[41] Ibid., p. 271.

[42] Ibid.

[43] Ibid., p. 279.

Sharahi Kanz al-Daqaiq

This commentary was written by Qawam al-Din Mas'ud bin Ibrahim Kirmani (d. AH 748).[44]

Sharah al-Maqdisi

It was written by 'Ali bin Muhammad al-Maqdisi (d. AH 1004).[45]

Hisam-ud-din Abu 'Abdullah Muhammad bin Muhammad Akhsikasi

Hisam-ud-din Abu 'Abdullah Muhammad bin Muhammad Akhsikasi (d. AH 644) was a native of Akhsikas, a famous town in Farghana Valley. He was born there in AH 572 in a pleasent scholarly atmosphere. The famous biographer Haji Khalifa holds the view that Akhsikas, during the Samanid regime remained a prestigious centre for the scholarly persuits and the jurists of this region contributed an immense share to the development of Islamic jurisprudence. This vicinity, even before the coming of Islam, reports the famous Muslim geographer, al-Maqdisi, has been a populous city of Mawara al-Nahr during fourth and fifth century CE.[46]

Akhsikasi acquired knowledge in various disciplines of the Islamic learning and distinguished himself as an eminent scholar in the field of Islamic jurisprudence. Among his famous teachers we can mention Fakhruddin Qazi Khan (d. AH 592) and Burhan al-Din 'Ali bin Abu Bakr Marghinani (d. AH 596), the prime-architects of the Islamic legal theory. The contribution of these scholars in the field of Islamic jurisprudence could never be underestimated. Both the personalities belong to Central Asia and have a dintinction in deducting legal notions from the basic and alternate sources of the law.[47]

44 Al-Qarshi, op. cit., vol. II, p. 193.

45 Haji Khalifah, op. cit., vol. III, p. 118.

46 Ibid., p. 219.

47 Al-Qarshi, op. cit., vol. I, p. 67.

تعلم يا بنى الفقه و العلم　　　و كن فى الفقه ذا جهد و رأى

و لا تكن مثل حبال تراه　　　إلى مر الزمان إلى و را ى

> O my son acquire Islamic jurisprudence and knowledge and become a reliable jurist and analyst, I have brought you up when you were as weak as an untied thread.[48]

Among his disciples include Muhammad bin 'Umar Nohabuzi, Muhammad al-Bukhari, Fakhrdin Muhammad bin Ahmad and Muhammad Ilyas Marghinani. These renowned figures as is conformed by their treatises, contributed in various capacities by associating themselves to the prestigious centres of learning in the medieval Central Asia.[49]

CONTRIBUTION

Akhsikasi approached various aspects of Islamic sciences and associated himself with the distinguished scholars held in great esteem. Akhsikasi's expertise include *tafsir* (Quranic exegesis), *'ilm al-kalam* (scholastic discourse), *mantiq* (logic), *tarikh* (history), *hadith* (prophetic traditions) and *fiqh* (jurisprudence). He compiled *Al-Fusul* a treatise in refutation to Al-Ghazali's *Mankhul* authored by Imam al-Ghazali (d. CE 1111) against the massive use of *qiyas* (analogy). The book, *Al-Fusul* has six chapters arranged authoritatively to depict the significance and legal techniques obtained and experienced through the *qiyas*.[50]

Besides the treatise *Al-Fusul,* Akhsikasi compiled *Muntakhab Hissami*, a renowned treatise carrying *usul al-fiqh*

---

48 Gangohi, op. cit., p. 277.

49 Ibid., p. 278.

50 Ibid.

(principles of Islamic jurisprudence). This work is still within the curricula of the Islamic seminaries throughout the Muslim world. The special feature of this treatise is its approach to deal with the subsequent techniques deployed in the field of Islamic jurisprudence. This work is considered as the primary source while approaching the selective works of the Hanafi methodology in *usul al-fiqh*.[51]

Commentaries of Muntakhab Hissami

The annotations and the commentaries compiled upon Akhsikasi's *Muntakhab Hissami* have elaborated various dimensions of the Islamic legal thought and formulated the possibility of unification of various schools of law in Islam. These commentaries again emphasize the validity of Akhsikasi's legal thought in order to understand the law in purview of the social context.

Sharah al-Muntakhab al-Hissami

This commentary was written by 'Abdullah bin Ahmad Nasafi (d. AH 710).[52]

Al-Wafi Sharah Muntakhab Hissami

This commentary was written by Husayn bin 'Ali Sun' anati (d. AH 711).[53]

Al-Tahqeeq

This commentary was written by 'Abd al-'Aziz bin Ahmad Bukhari (d. AH 730).[54]

---

51 Haji Khalifah, op. cit., vol. III, p. 221.

52 Ibid., p. 221.

53 Ibid., p. 223.

54 Umar Raza Kahalah, *Mujam al-Mualifin*, Damascus, 1957, vol. II, p. 164.

Taby'ien

This commentary was written by Qawam bin 'Amir Katib al-Itiqani (d. AH 758). He completed this commentary in AH 716 at the time he performed the holy pilgrimage (Hajj). The celebrated scholar of *usul al-fiqh,* Abd al-'Aziz Bukhari (d. AH 730) holds the view that Itiqani's *sharah* (commentary) is an extraordinary masterpiece for those interested in the study of *usul al-fiqh.*[55]

Tahqeeq bar Muntakhab

This commentary was written by Ahmad bin 'Uthman Turkmani (d. AH 744).[56]

Sharah Muntakhab al-Muttawal

This work was compiled by 'Abdullah bin Ahmad Nasafi (d. AH 710).[57]

Hashiya

This work was compiled by Mo'inuddin Imrani (d. AH 877).[58]

Taleem al-'Aami fi Tashreeh al-Hissami

This commentary was written by Barkatullah bin Muhammad Lakhnavi.[59]

Taleeq al-Haami 'ala al-Hissami

This commentary was written by Faiz al-Hassan Gangohi.[60]

---

55 Gangohi, op. cit., p. 287.

56 Ibid., p. 288.

57 Umar Raza Kahalah, op. cit., p. 167.

58 Haji Khalifah, op. cit., vol. III, p. 121.

59 Gangohi, op. cit., p. 288.

60 Ibid.

Al-Nami Sharah al-Hissami

This commentary was written by Muhammad 'Abd al-Haq Dehalavi.[61]

Najmuddin Abu Hafs 'Umar bin Muhammad al-Nasafi

The celebrated scholar Najmuddin Abu Hafs 'Umar bin Muhammad al-Nasafi was born in "Nasf", in AH 461. In course of its academic excellence, Nasf has been a prestigious centre of the Islamic learning in Mawara al-Nahr during the Abbasid (CE 750–1258) and Samanid regimes (CE 874–1005). Muhammad al-Nasafi was an eminent scholar whose contribution to the Muslim intellectualism has been so much overwhelming. He was a versatile figure who contributed a remarkable share to various branches of the Islamic sciences including *tafsir, hadith, fiqh* and *mantiq*. As per the historical accounts this grand scholar acquired his knowledge by travelling to reputed centres of the Islamic learning in Mawara al-Nahr, Arabia and Iraq. These travels proved to be so dynamic that he came to be identified as a meritorious scholar among his contemporaries. Moreover, he tried to equip himself with almost all the literary and methodological trends in the Islamic knowledge system existed at that time. In the given context, al-Nasafi approached the field of Islamic jurisprudence and excelled over his contemporaries by adding some valuable notions while commenting on the Islamic legal theory. It is worth to mention here that the region Mawara al-Nahr, during fifth century AH, was famous for a number of jurists who had a commendable expertise in the field of *takhrij* (legal deduction) and *istehsan* (public good). These juristic instruments have been deployed to deduce the legal stuff from the primary and secondary sources of law in light of the approved human reason.[62]

---

[61] Gangohi, op. cit., p. 289.

[62] Ibn Qatlubigah, *Taj al-Tarajim fi Tabaqat al-Hanafiyah*, Baghdad, 1962, p. 162.

Among al-Nasafi's teachers we can mention Muhammad al-Buzudi (d. AH 493) and Imam al-Sarakhsi (d. AH 490) whose critical approach and absolute acquaintance with the legal theory are still unparallel. Both the personalities had a distinction and command in the methodology of *usul al-fiqh*. Al-Nasafi in his record of teachers, entitled *T'idat al-Shayukh al-Umar* speaks high of both the experts and adds the title *hujjat* (authority) to their name.[63] It was ultimately due to the influence and impact of such renowned figures that al-Nasafi emerged as an eminent figure in Islamic jurisprudence. Al-Nasafi, as depicted by his approach, remained a distinguished scholar who could interpret the relevant themes of Quran and Sunnah by way of socio-legal dimensions. Muhammad al-Nasafi surpassed his contemporaries by his commendable approach, critical sense and on spot resolution of the issues. By proper understanding of *'illat* (reason) and application of the required legal aid, he has always been appreciated by his teachers and contemporaries. Al-Nasafi's teachers, as reported by 'Umar Raza Kahalah, one and all treated him as *imam* (the grand jurist) whose juristic explanations and references were approached and quoted by the jurists of Iraq and Syria.[64]

Al-Nasafi was a jurist *par excellence*. His approach to understand the dimensions of a socio-legal issue and ability to discover henceforth implications was widely appreciated. The Hanafi scholars, to authenticate their argument, narrated from his treatises for decades together. In the realm of Hanafi jurisprudence al-Nasafi is considered to be an eminent authority who could utilize the optimum social evidences as the source of law. Being a noted scholar, his legal expertise was so vibrant that the possibility of difference within Islam (*ikhtilaf fi-al-masalik*) could easily be understood. Al-Nasafi's

---

[63] Gangohi, op. cit., p. 295.

[64] Zarkali, *Al-A'lam*, Beirut, 1953, vol. II, p. 138.

practical approach in this direction equipped the legal theory to advance towards an effective interaction between law and the society.[65] Al-Nasafi gathered around him a good number of scholars who made a valuable addition to the juristic thought in Mawara al-Nahr. Among his calibred disciples included his eldest son, Abu Laith Nasr bin Muhammad bin Ahmad, 'Ali bin Abu Bakr Marghinani, 'Abdul 'Aziz Balkhi, Muhammad bin Jaleel al-Samarqandi, Ahmad bin Muhammad Khawarizmi, Ahmad bin Musa al-Kashti and Muhammad bin Hassan al-Kasani.[66]

Al-Nasafi consolidated the entire structure of the Islamic jurisprudence and improved upon the advances achieved by the early jurists. He died in Samarkand in AH 537, leaving behind him a marvellous contribution in terms of scholarship as well as profound disciples who expounded innovative expertise maintaining the standards of the Islamic legal thought.

CONTRIBUTION

Najmuddin Abu Hafs 'Umar bin Muhammad al-Nasafi is known for his profound scholarship in Islamic jurisprudence and at least 105 treatises are credited to him compiled in various disciplines of Islamic sciences. This utmost concern for promoting the knowledge tradition in Islam narrates his zeal as well as undisputed worth regarding certain fields of knowledge.[67] The renowned Muslim biographer and historian Haji Khalifa has attributed to him the following works:[68]

Al-Taysir fi 'Ilm al-Tafasir

This credible work was compiled in the field of *tafsir* (Quranic

---

65 Gangohi, op. cit., p. 294.

66 N.J. Coulson, *A History of Islamic Law*, Edinburgh, 1990, p. 37.

67 Haji Khalifah, op. cit., vol. IV, p. 273.

68 Nasafi, *Al-Qand fi Zikr al-Ulema al-Samarqand*, Saudi Arabia, 1987, p. 312.

exegesis) to facilitate and explore various dimensions of the *tafsir* methodology, revelation and its social application.[69]

Al-Manzumah

This work is also a commendable treatise on *fiqh* written in poetic style (*Nazm*).[70]

Nazm al-Jami al-Sagir

This work is a valuable commentary on al-Shayabani's reputed work *Jami al-Sagir.*[71]

Al-Qand fi Zikr-i-Ulama-i-Samarqand

This treatise is an encyclopaedic masterpiece unfolding the venture of various Islamic disciplines along biography of the scholars of Samarkand and Mawara al-Nahr. Its recent edition appeared from Lebanon and was also published by Maktaba al-Kausar, Saudi Arabia in 1987.[72]

Kitab al-Mawaqit

This work is a brief account carrying necessary information and description on *salah* (prayers) and *thaum* (fasting).[73]

Al-Ahsar bi al-Mukhtar

This work has been compiled to deal with *al-fatawa al-mutafariqah* (decrees concerning miscellaneous legal issues).[74]

Mashar-i-Sharayah

This treatise is the summation and explanation of some of the

[69] Haji Khalifah, op. cit., vol. IV, p. 374.

[70] Ibid., p. 374.

[71] Ibid., p. 375.

[72] Ibid., p. 373.

[73] Ibn Qatlubigah, op. cit., p. 165.

[74] Ibid., p. 166.

critical legal discourses to examine the nature of rulings deducted for the alternate sources of law.[75]

Kitab al-Shurat

This book is mainly related to the study of *khiyar* (law of options) and is a valuable treatise to understand the phenomenon of *al-mamalat al-iqtisadiyah* (commercial contracts).[76]

Talba al-Talba

This treatise explains and examines various modes of the analogy in Islamic law. The content of the book is really critical as it elaborates the major works of the early Hanafi jurists who formulated the legal discourse during the early phase.[77]

Tarikh-i-Bukahara

This work is a valuable treatise to envision the history, contribution and literary developments in Bukhara during various political regimes.[78]

Al-'Aqaid al-Nasafiyah

This treatise is Nasafi's most popular work in the field of *kalam* (scholastic discourse and philosophy). Al-Nasafi highlights, in this treatise the significance of faith-based scholastic discourse, the faculty of doubt and its limitations. The celebrated author defends the Islamic belief system against infidelity and refutes the Greek logic and their logical interpretations by strong argumentation.[79]

Ijalat al-Hasabi bi Sana'at al-Mughrabi

This compilation is a valuable commentary of the precepts

---

75 Gangohi, op. cit., p. 296.

76 Ibid., p. 295.

77 Ibid., p. 297.

78 Ibid., p. 298.

79 Haji Khalifah, op. cit., vol. IV, p. 372.

carrying importance of language for juristic discourse. The book unveils the significance of logic and explains as how to resolve the critical issues encountered by the society in the absence of a textual verdict.[80]

Al-Fatawah al-Nasafiyah

This reputed work is a compilation of decrees authored in connection with various socio-religious issues. Al-Nasafi catagorized the legal verdicts and introduced the concept of *qawanin* which emphasizes the social content as a source of law hence can be explored for the deduction of legal instruments in absence of revealed *ahkam*.[81]

Kitab al-Najah fi Sharah al-Akhbar al-Sitah

This work is also a *magnum opus* compiled by al-Nasafi in the field of *hadith*. This treatise deals with the works and commentaries authored upon the *sihah al-sittah* (six authentic books of *hadith*). The work also examines the narrations repeatedly used and acknowledged by the famous *muhadithin* (traditionists) while compiling their works.[82]

Among the works compiled by al-Nasafi, *Al-'Aqaid al-Nasafiyah* is still considered as an unparallel, authoritative and much creative work in the field of scholastic discourse. This book has been annotated by eminent scholars to benefit the learners as well as the scholarly community. The famous commentaries written to this monumental work include:

1. *Sharah al-'Aqaid* compiled by Muhammad bin Ahmad Asphahani (d. AH 759).[83]

---

80 Zarkali, op. cit., vol. II, p. 141.

81 Ibid., p. 286.

82 Ibn Khalikan, *Wafiyat al-A'yan*, Beruit, 1977, vol. I, p. 56.

83 Ibid., p. 57.

2. *Al-'Aqaid Ala al-'Aqaid* compiled by Sheikh Mehmud bin Ahmad Qunavi (d. AH 770).[84]
3. *Sharah al-'Aqaid* compiled by Sa'ad din Taftazani (d. AH 792).[85]
4. *Al-Ruddah* compiled by Ibn Hazm al-Andulusi (d. AH 1064).[86]
5. *Al-Qual al-Wafi li-Sharh-i-'Aqaid al-Nasafi* compiled by Muhammad bin Zainuddin (d. AH 783).[87]
6. *Al-Fawaid al-Qadriyah fi Sharah-i-'Aqaid al-Nasafiyah* compiled by 'Abdul Qadir Silhati (d. AH 1004).[88]
7. *Hil al-Qa'id fi Sharah al-'Aqaid* commentary by Mulla Zadah Haravi (d. AH 891).[89]

Abu al-Hassan 'Ali bin Muhammad al-Bazudi

Sheikh al-Islam Abu al-Hassan 'Ali bin Muhammad al-Bazudi is among such great jurists whose stature and contribution will be remembered for all times to come. He was born in Bazud, a veteran village in Mawara al-Nahr in AH 400. The village Bazud shares its neighbourhood with Nasf which is located six miles eastwards from it. As reported by the prominent Muslim historians, Bazud has been a prominent centre for Islamic learning and a good number of great figures emerged from its soil. These reputed luminaries did a lot for the promotion of Islamic knowledge and enhanced the spectrum of Islamic intellectualism for centuries together. It was particularly during the Samanid period (CE 874–1105), that this entire region reached the zenith of progress and contributed an immense share to

[84] Ibn Khalikan, *Wafiyat al-A'yan*, Beruit, 1977, vol. I, p. 58.

[85] Nasafi, op. cit., p. 318.

[86] Ibid.

[87] Ibn Khalikan, op. cit., vol. I, p. 59.

[88] Ibid.

[89] Gangohi, op. cit., p. 295.

various dimensions of the socio-intellectual aspect. Due to its pleasant scholarly atmosphere, it remained a great hub for the intellectual activities and was known for academic environment among the cities of Mawara al-Nahr.[90]

'Ali bin Muhammad al-Bazudi's grandfather Abd al-Karim, as holds al-Qarshi, was a learned and most intelligent disciple of Abu Mansur Samarqandi (d. AH 318), a distinguished and eminent scholar in the field of Islamic jurisprudence. Ultimately, it was this virtuous upkeep that nourished al-Bazudi as an eminent figure among his contemporaries. Fakhr al-Islam Bazudi has always been remembered as the principal authority in the Islamic legal with a great hold upon all the possible instruments for the deduction of law. He as a theorist in this field compiled works on doctrinal principles (*al-Usul al-Fiqh*) and expounded the discourse of the *fatawa* methodology. After acquiring knowledge in different branches of learning, he spent twelve years in Bukhara and Samarkand to equip himself with sound and reliable materials available at that time. His versatile expertise and authority over the subject made him an unparalled scholar and the scholars gathered around him to obtain the maximum benefit out of his research and legal expertise. Imam Bazudi, as an eminent jurist, looked and searched into the alternate legal instruments and formulated the theory of *maakhaz al-farai'ah* (alternate deductions) in the issues not touched or explored by the primary sources of law.[91] He is reported to have utilized the subject matter of Quran and prophetic traditions as a guiding force to advance towards much balanced legal deductions. His profound scholarship and juristic skill broadened the horizon of *qiyas* and its role in formulation of the theory as well as to understand the exigent circumstances.[92]

---

[90] Ibn Al-Athir, *Al-Kamil fi al-Tarikh*, Labenon, 1987, vol. II, p. 79.

[91] Abu al-Hai Lucknawi, *Al-Fawaid al-Bahiyah*, Delhi, AH 1311, p. 192.

[92] Al-Qarshi, op. cit., vol. I, p. 219.

Imam Bazudi, as a reputed jurist, made valuable additions to *'ilm al-fatawa* by writing its basic principles, urgencies and modes of operating upon the judgements reported from his predecessors. Marghinani (d. AH 593) in his celebrated work, *al-Hidayah* has exclusively made references from his principal work *al-Usul* while dealing with the issues concerning *masa'il al-wadiah* (commercial deposits) and *masa'il al-wakalah* (laws of agencies).[93]

Fakhr al-Islam Bazudi revolutionized the field of Islamic jurisprudence especially by the systematic concepts of *al-tajziyah* (analysis) and *al-tashbiyah* (similitude) which he considered to be the monumental in the course of *qiyas* (analogy) and *ijma* (consensus). Imam Bazudi's legal techniques to resolve the socio-religious issues have also been incredible. Imam al-Bazudi holds the view that the concepts of *al-tajziyah* and *al-tashbiyah* can facilitate an advance to make the law relevant to the changing circumstances.[94]

Imam al-Bazudi, living a busy scholarly and spiritual life, died in Samarkand in AH 482 leaving behind him a galaxy of eminent disciples and delicate works that affirm his profound scholarship and expertise in the field of Islamic jurisprudence.[95]

CONTRIBUTION

Fakhr al-Islam Bazudi laid the foundation of systematic analogy in an integrated, thorough and discern manner. His approach, while approaching the alternate sources of law, was much closer to the spirit of Quran and Sunnah. To facalitate and devise the course of *fiqh* methodology, Imam al-Bazudi reached the conclusion that al-Shayabani's and Imam Shafi's works carry the basic stuff required for the study of the

---

93 Al-Marghinani, *Al-Hidayah,* Delhi, 1925, vol. II, p. 109.

94 Karkhi, *Risalah fi Ilm al-Usul,* Cairo, 1922, p. 19.

95 Gangohi, op. cit., p. 567.

formulation of the legal theory of Islam. Al-Bazudi's keen insight and worth to put forth a set of selective principles have been a hallmark in the history of Islamic jurisprudence. Al-Bazudi annotated al-Shayabani's two celebrated works *Jami al-Sagir* and *Jami al-Kabir* for the proper understanding of juristic instruments deployed to deduct the rulings for the exigent circumstances. The famous biographer and analyst of the experts of *ilm al-usul*, Abd al-'Ali writes:

و تلك العبارات كأنها صخر مركوزة فيها الجواهر و أوراق مستورة فيها الزواهر تحيرت أصحاب الأذهان الثاقبة فى أخذ معانيها و قنع الغائصون فى بحارها بالأصداف عن الأليها و لا أستحى من الحق و أقول قو ل الصدق: انجل كلامه العظيم لا قدر على حله إلا من نال فضله الجسيم و أعطى الله له قلب سليم .

> And those (juristic) statements are as strong as rocks, decorated by rubies, or (they are to be compared with) leaves with flowers. Even intelligent people astonish to seek their meanings. The scholars sunk in deep oceans of these statements and confine themselves only to oysters. And I never hesitate in saying truth and honestly say that only those could get reward of his venture that have received a part from Almighty's blessings and have attained from Him (Almighty) a calibred heart.[96]

The noted biographer, commentrator and jurist, 'Allama Tashkubrazadah (d. AH 962), refers to him as the most authoritative, reliable and intelligent among his contemporaries. His legal expertise was extremely authentic and valuable regarding the law of Islam:

فخر الإسلام محمد البزودى مشهور بأبى العسر لعسر تصنيفاته

[96] 'Abd al-'Ali, *Sharah Musalam al-Thabut*, Hyderabad, AH 1368, p. 72.

> Fakhr al-Islam Bazudi has been famous as Abi al-'Usr (father of complication) due of his delicate treatises.[97]

Imam al-Bazudi has to his credit the following works which he compiled in the various disciplines of Islamic sciences:

Tafsir al-Quran

Imam al-Bazudi wrote a commendable Quranic exegeses entitled, *Tafsir al-Quran,* which is considered to be his principal work in the field of *Tafsir*. Bazudi followed Zamakhsheri's (d. AH 467) style and annotated Quranic verses by minimizing the differences between *wahy* (revelation) and *'aql* (reason). This commentary, appeared in several volumes and got recognition for its style of argumentation and rationality.[98]

Al-Mabsut

Al-Mabsut is one of the reputed works compiled by Imam al-Bazudi. He compiled this work during his stay in Samarkand. This work was authored to sum up the basic derivatives and instruments that were generally adopted and elaborated by the jurists. The main sources to this treatise were *fatawas*, *mubahs* and *usul* put forth by Imam al-Shayabani (d. AH 189) and Imam Abu Yusuf while discussing the scope and sources of the Islamic legal theory.[99]

Kanz al-Usul 'ala Ma'rifat al-Usul

Kanz al-Usul 'ala Ma'rifat al-Usul is Imam al-Bazudi's reputed work compiled in the field of *usul al-fiqh* (principles of Islamic jurisprudence). The main feature of this juristic work is its flexible and rational characteristics that mark its distinction in all the schools of Islamic jurisprudence. Its method of the

---

[97] Tashkubrazadah, *Miftah al-Sa'adah*, Cairo, 1935, p. 209.

[98] Ibn Khalikan, op. cit., vol. III, p. 113.

[99] Ibid., vol. II, p. 108.

legal deductions added splendour to the Hanafi School of Law and widened its scope for the intellectual urgency.[100]

Sharah Jam'i al-Sagir

Shah Jam'i al-Sagir is the annotation and commentary of Shayabani's *Jami al-Sagir* in order to get the maximum benefit out of his profound scholarship.[101]

Sharah Jam'i al-Kabir

Fakhr al-Islam Bazudi has also made a valuable commentary on Shayabani's *Jam'i al-Kabir*. Imam al-Bazudi examined, elaborated and explained the methodological principles of Hanafi School of Law in order to make a distinctive analytical study of Imam al-Shayabani's scholarship.[102]

Ghina al-Fuquha

Ghina al-Fuquha compiled by Imam al-Bazudi is a valuable and reputed work carrying the guiding principles of legalization, etiquettes of *qaza* and a manual highlighting the causes for the emergence of systematic reasoning in Islamic jurisprudence.[103]

Sharah al-Bukhari

Fakhr al-Islam Bazudi approached Muhammad bin Isma'il Bukhari's (d. AH 256) celebrated work *al-Jami al-Sahih* and wrote its commentary *Sharah* to make a proper understanding of *ahadith* in the given context. This reputed work conforms Imam al-Bazudi's profound scholarship and expertise in the field of *hadith* as well.[104]

---

100 *Dairah al-Ma'arif*, op. cit., 1884, vol. I, p. 688.

101 Ibid., p. 681.

102 Ibid., p. 683.

103 Ibid., p. 687.

104 Tashkubrazadah, op. cit., p. 216.

Kitab al-Imali

Kitab al-Imali, compiled by Fakhr al-Islam Bazudi, is a valuable record of *riwayat* (narrations) and *masmu'at* (hearings) dictated to him by his teachers and contemporaries. These narrations, as referred by the authentic sources, have been attributed to Imam Abu Hanifa, Imam Abu Yusuf and Imam al-Shayabani. This legal stuff, in due course of time, reached the learners and disciples who carried it along the regions of Iraq and Mawara al-Nahr.[105]

Sa'ad din Mas'ud bin 'Umar Taftazani

The grand jurist Imam Sa'ad din Mas'ud bin 'Umar Taftazani was a renowned figure, Central Asia has ever produced. Although he wrote in almost all the disciplines of Islamic sciences, his basic field of expertise was Islamic jurisprudence to which he contributed throughout his life. He was born in Taftazan in AH 722, in the vicinity of Mawara al-Nahr, currently within the territory of Uzbekistan. Imam al-Taftazani is considered among the prime figures that played a vital role in disseminating the knowledge of Islamic jurisprudence in this region. He mastered in different branches of Islamic sciences and compiled authoritative treatises in Islamic sciences including logic and philosophy. Imam al-Taftazani's importance lies in the fact that he compiled the decrees of prominent jurists of Mawara al-Nahr, discussed their nature, examined their limitations and discovered their relevance. It is mainly due to his authority in *ilm al-kalam* (scholastic discourse) that his commentary on Nasafi's (d. AH 710) *al-'Aqaid* is still considered to be the most valuable anecdotes in *fiqh al-Akbar*. Haji Khalifa affirms his scholarship:

> Taftazani surpassed his contemporaries and the jurists and scholars got benefited from his writings, lectures and discussions for next three centuries.[106]

---

[105] Gangophi, op. cit., p. 567.

[106] Haji Khalifah, op. cit., vol. IV, p. 403.

Sa'ad din Masu'd bin 'Umar Taftazani acquired his knowledge from the reputed scholars 'Azudin and Qutb udin Razi, two significant and noted figures at that time. Both the scholars are known for their valuable contribution in the field of *usul al-fiqh* and have been referred as the pride of their age. As a matter of fact, Imam al-Taftazani was much influenced by 'Azudin, who had been a critical, decisive and keen observer regarding Taftazani's interest in the field of Islamic jurisprudence. The intense care of the teachers, his zeal and ultimate concern in legal discourse established him as an authority in Islamic knowledge system. Imam al-Taftazani gave valid explorations to identify reason as an approved source for the deduction of legal verdicts.[107]

After acquiring the knowledge of various branches of learning, Taftazani made a successful attempt to concentrate upon the legal discourses and tried to interpret legality of the *'Urf* (social practice) as a source of law in Islam. This he did to make the legal injunctions relevant to the social circumstances. In this learned venture, his disciples especially 'Abd al-Wasi bin Khazr, Shams-uddin Muhammad bin Ahmad, Burhan-uddin Haider, Ibrahim Haravi, Jalal-uddin Yusuf also contributed to set new standards in the study of Islamic law.[108]

A noted historian, Syed Ahmad Tahtavi says:

انتهت عليه رئاسة الحنفية في زمنه

At him ends the Hanafite leadership in his time.[109]

---

[107] *Encyclopaedia of Islam*, vol. IV, p. 508.

[108] Abu Hai Lucknawi, op. cit., p. 168.

[109] Ibid., p. 179.

Kufavi, a famous biographer, shares the view and makes his account as:

كان من محاسن الزمان ،لم تر العيون مثله فى الأعلام و الاعيان

> He was a blessing on time. Eyes never saw his example among scholars and learned.[110]

Imam al-Taftazani passed away on 22 Muharram AH 792 in Samarkand and his date of death has been depicted in this Persian couplet:[111]

عقل را بير سيدم از تاريخ سال رحلتش   كفت تاريخش يك كم طيب الله ثراه

> Taftazani's son Muhammad (d. AH 838) has been also a great figure who compiled *Tehzib al-Mantiq wa-al-Kalam* which is still considered to be a monumental work in the field of philosophy.[112]

CONTRIBUTION

Imam Sa'ad din Mas'ud bin 'Umar Taftazani is credited with the following works:

Sharah Tasrif Zinjani

Sharah Tasrif Zinjani is Taftazani's first work which was compiled in AH 738 during his stay in Tirmiz.[113]

Muttawal

The book *Muttawal* was compiled in AH 748 in Herat.[114]

---

110 Abu Hai Lucknawi, op. cit., p. 178.

111 Ibid., p. 180.

112 Ibid., pp. 170-71.

113 Gangohi, op. cit., p. 417.

114 Ibid.

Mukhtasar al-Ma'ani

This work by Taftazani is considered to be a reputed treatise on scholastic discourses compiled in AH 756.[115]

Sadiya Sharah Shamsiyah

This work was compiled in Mazar-i-Jam in AH 757.[116]

Talvih

This work is a valuable addition to the field of *usul al-fiqh* written by Taftazani during his stay in Turkistan in AH 758.[117]

Sharah Aqaid al-Nasafia

This work was compiled in AH 768.[118]

Mukhtasir al-Usul

This work is a reputed edition in Islamic jurisprudence, compiled in Samarkand in AH 770.[119]

Al-Irshad

This treatise is based on the decrees issued by Taftazani during his stay in Khawarizm in AH 774.[120]

Maqasid

This book was compiled in Samarkand in AH 784. Taftazani himself wrote its commentary entitled *Sharah al-Maqasid*.[121]

---

115 Haji Khalifah, op. cit., vol. IV, p. 428.

116 Ibid., p. 418.

117 Ibid., p. 419.

118 Gangohi, op. cit., p. 417.

119 Ibid.

120 Ibid., p. 419.

121 Haji Khalifah, op. cit., vol. IV, p. 431.

Tehzib al-Mantiq wa-al-Kalam

This work was compiled in AH 789 in Bukhara. It is a compilation authored in the field of logic and scholistic discourse.[122]

Sharah Miftah al-Ulum

Taftazani compiled this work during his stay in Samarkand in AH 789. The special feature of this work is that the celebrated author narrated significance of various aspects of knowledge and necessitated for the study of logic and jurisprudence.[123]

Sharah Hadith al-Arba'in

This treatise is a commentary on forty authentic *ahadiths* of Prophet Muhammad (SAW).[124]

Risalah al-Ikrah

This work is a famous pamphlet by Taftazani based on the decrees related to the laws of compulsion.[125]

Kashf al-Asrar

This treatise is Taftazani's famous commentary on Holy Quran authored in Persian language.[126]

Sharah Muntaha al-Sawal wa al-'Aml fi 'Ilm al-Usul

This book is a reputed treatise heightening the legal instruments that serve as the basic principles of Islamic jurisprudence.[127]

---

122 Haji Khalifah, op. cit., vol. IV, p. 428.

123 Ibid., p. 431.

124 Ibid.

125 Ibid., p. 432.

126 Ibid., p. 433.

127 Ibid., p. 434.

Nim al-Sawabig fi Sharah al-Nawabig

This work is a valuable record of the rare discourses and much complicated issues related to the legal philosophy of Islam.[128]

Rislah fi Tahqiq al-Yaman

This work is a scholarly contribution debating nature of the issues related to the laws of trusts and vows.[129]

Fatawa Hanafiyah

This work by Taftazani is a valuable account of the decrees issued by reputed Hanafi jurists and serves as the ready reference to resolve the socio-religious issues. This book was compiled at Herat in AH 769.[130]

Miftah al-Fiqh

This treatise is a dictionary of the terms often used in Islamic jurisprudence. Taftazani elaborated *mustalahat* (the *fiqh* terminology) to explain its significance in day-to-day life.[131]

Hashiyah al-Kashaf

Taftazani made a superb attempt to compile a commentary on famous exegesis of Quran, *Tafsir al-Kashaf* by Zamakhshari, but unfortunately remained incomplete due to his ill health.[132]

Sharah al-Hidayah

During last months of his life, Taftazani had an idea of annotating Marghinani's (d. AH 593) *al-Hidayah*. It is also reported that he wrote the commentary over the beginning chapters but this work remained incomplete due his sudden

---

128 Haji Khalifah, op. cit., vol. IV, p. 435.

129 Ibid., p. 436.

130 Ibid., p. 437.

131 Ibid., p. 452.

132 Ibid., p. 449.

death in AH 792 in Samarkand.[133]

Razi al-din Hassan bin Muhammad al-Saghani

The grand scholar and jurist Razi al-din Hassan bin Muhammad al-Saghani was a native of Saghan (Chagan) a famous village near Merv in Mawara al-Nahr. He was born there in AH 577 and this entire region, as the sources tell us has been a hub of knowledge and renowned figures flourished there during sixth century AH. After acquiring knowledge in different branches of Islamic learning from Mawara al-Nahr, he travelled to distant parts of the Muslim world to equip himself with the latest trends as well as to gain more expertise into the various dimensions of *'ulum* (Islamic sciences). In the given context, he remained in Ghaznah for two years, visited Baghdad in AH 615 and learned under reputed scholars pertaining to various disciplines of the Islamic knowledge. Al-Saghani was deputed to India (al-Hind) by the later Abbasid caliphs in about AH 617/CE 1215 as an ambassador of the Islamic caliphate to have an interaction with the Mumluk Sultans of Delhi. With this extraordinary mission, he played a significant role in developing inter-caliphate relations. It has also been mentioned by the contemporary historians, and thus he contributed as an eminient diplomat as well.[134]

To benefit from the expertise of the scholars of Hejaz (Arabia), Razi al-din Hassan bin Muhammad al-Saghani visited Makkah in AH 632 and throughout this stay he enriched himself with emblematic, technical and latest trends in *hadith* and *fiqh* literature. He involved himself with scholarly circles of different schools of thought and succeeded in gaining an excellent legal understanding of the juristic differences. Ultimately, the peculiar nature of the Hanafi School of Law

---

133 Haji Khalifah, op. cit., vol. IV, p. 452.

134 Riaz al-Islam, *Indo-Persian Relations*, Tehran, 1970, p. 62.

impressed him much to comprehend the socio-political and legal problems. In AH 633, al-Saghani performed the Hajj and travelled to Yemen to equip and reorient himself with Arab rhetoric and eloquence. After gaining a blissful expertise in the Arabic lexicon he returned to Baghdad and was received with honour by the Abbasid caliph. Al-Saghani revisited India in AH 637 and remained here for some time. During this stay he approached Sanskrit language and gained mastery over this language within months. Al-Saghani has recorded several anecdotes of the Indian folklore, mythology and culture, and carried it to Baghdad in AH 639. During his visit to different Muslim lands he prepared masterpieces in both Arabic and Persian literature in addition to the field of Islamic jurisprudence.[135]

Al-Saghani was a jurist *par excellence*. The famous Indian scholar, Abu al-Hai Lakhnavi, affirms his contribution in these words:

كان فقيها ،محدثا ،لغويا ذا مشاركة تامة فى جميع العلوم

> He was a jurist, traditionist and lexicographer having profound scholarship in various sciences.[136]

The noted biographer, Sayyuti praises him and holds the view:

هو حامل لواء اللغة و الفقه فى زمانه

> He was an authority in Arabic lexicon and jurisprudence during his times.[137]

Razi al-din Hassan bin Muhammad al-Saghani has been the contemporary of the reputed Indian Sufi Nizam al-din Aulia

---

[135] Riaz al-Islam, *Indo-Persian Relations*, Tehran, 1970, p. 63.

[136] Abu al-Hai Lucknawi, op. cit., p. 167.

[137] Gangohi, op. cit., p. 558.

(d. CE 1238). Alauddin Amir Sanjari, a disciple of Nizam al-din Aulia, had compiled a collection of his letters entitled *Fawaid al-Fawaid* which mentions al-Saghani's intellectual stature as well as his scholarship in these words:

دران ایام در حضرت دهلی علماء کبار بوند با ا ین همه (الصاغانی) در علوم

مستاوی بود اما در علم حدیث از همه ممتاز و هیج کس مقابل او نبود

> During those days, Delhi contained great scholars, Saghani was equivalent to them, but al-Saghani was an authority in *hadith* and nobody could combat him.[138]

Nizam al-din Aulia himself admits the fact and holds:

اگر حدیث براد مشکل شدی رسول الله صلی الله علیہ وسلم را در خواب دیدی و صحیح کردی.

> If he would face any sort of difficulty in *hadith*, Prophet Muhammad (SAW) would appear (in dream) and remove that difficulty.[139]

Razi al-din Saghani died in Baghdad during the reign of Abbasid Caliph Mustasim in AH 650 and was buried in Mecca as per his will.[140]

إن لله عبادا فطنا　　طلقوا الدنيا و خافوا الفتنا

نظروا فيها فلما علموا　　أنها ليست لحى وطنا

جعلوها لجة و اتخذوا　　صالح الأعمال فيها سفنا "

> Verily Allah's servants devote themselves to Him only, they

138 Sanjari, *Fawaid al-Fawaid*, Istanbul, p. 321.

139 Ibid., p. 322.

140 Gangohi, op. cit., p. 558.

> depart from world and fear its indulgences. They looked into it (world) and ultimately found that it is not a permanent station (for them). They made it (world) a temporary place and declared righteousness a boat to cross this dark ocean.[141]

CONTRIBUTION

Razi al-din Hassan bin Muhammad Saghani authored a wide range of rare treatises in almost all the aspects of Islamic sciences. These books confirm his profound scholarship in diverse branches of knowledge and rank him among the renowned intellectuals of the Muslim world. An elaboration of some of the treatises is given here.

Mashariq al-Anwar

Mashariq al-Anwar al-Nabawiyah min Sihah al-Akhbar al-Mustafwiyah is a magnificent and vigorous compilation by Imam Saghani in the field of *hadith*. This valuable compilation was compiled in Baghdad. This reputed work was compiled as per the advice of the Abbasid caliph, Mustansir Billah making an account of 2,246 *ahadith* of *sahihain* (Bukhari and Muslim). The work has been so charming that the caliph himself learned this book from the reputed author.[142]

Kitab al-'Ubab

This book serves the purpose for knowing the appropriate meaning and usage of the Arabic phrases.[143]

Misbah al-Duja min Ahadith al-Mustafa

This valuable treatise is based on the *ahadith* pertaining to *mu'ashirah* (family and social dealings) of the day-to-day life.[144]

---

141 Imam Navawi, *Riaz al-Salihin*, Beirut, 1982, p. 5.

142 Gangohi, op. cit., p. 559.

143 Ibn Khalikan, op. cit., vol. III, p. 218.

144 Ibid., p. 219.

Al-Shamas al-Munirah min Sihah al-Mathurah

This compilation covers the basic juristic themes mentioned in the prophetic traditions. The work emphasizes the authority of Sunnah for the deduction of legal verdicts.[145]

Durat al-Sahabah fi wafiyat al-Sahabah

This book is a considerable treatise based on the biography of the celebrated companions of the Holy Prophet (SAW).[146]

Sharah Bukhari

This book is an annotation on *Jami al-Sahih al-Bukhari* of Muhammad bin Isma'il al-Bukhari (d. AH 256).[147]

Majma al-Bahrain

This is a comprehensive book comprising of fourteen volumes. A masterpiece in Arab lexicography ever authored in this style.[148]

Kitab al-Shawarid

This book is also a valuable addition to Arabic elocution.[149]

Kitab al-Ifti'al

This book is a treatise on Arabic grammar. The manuscript is currently preserved in the National Museum of Yemen.[150]

Kitab al-'Aruz

This magnificent work on Arabic grammar and poetry is a brief description of the rules and instruments deployed in the couplets.[151]

---

145 Ibn Khalikan, op. cit., vol. III, p. 221.

146 Gangohi, op. cit., p. 560.

147 Abu al-Hai Lucknawi, op. cit., p. 172.

148 Ibid., p. 174.

149 Gangohi, op. cit., p. 559.

150 Ibid., p. 558.

151 Ibid., p. 559.

Kitab al-Nawadir fi Lughat wa al-Tarkib

This celebrated work helps us to understand the basic mode of Arabic lexicon and eloquence.[152]

Zubdat al-Manasik

This treatise is a guide book and description of the obligatory notions involved in performing the *Hajj* and its etiquettes.[153]

Kitab al-Faraiz

This book is the description of the injunctions regarding the property shares mentioned in Quran and Sunnah.[154]

Darajat al-'Ilm wa al-'Ulama

Al-Saghani compiled this celebrated work to present Islamic concept of epistemology and role of the scholars and intellectuals who protect its domains. The work has been prepared from relevant Quranic verses and *ahadith* of the Prophet Muhammad (SAW) highlighting the fundamentals of the theory of knowledge in Islam.[155]

Kitab al-Asma al-Farah, Kitab al-Asma al-Asad and Kitab al-Asma al-Ziab

These booklets carry the meaning of the words commonly used for mouse, lion and wolf. The author has differentiated these words by taking age factor of these animals into consideration.[156]

Bagyat al-Sadyan

This book is a collection of the decrees and injunctions

---

152 Gangohi, op. cit., p. 559.

153 Abu al-Hai Lucknawi, op. cit., p. 177.

154 Haji Khalifah, op. cit., vol. III, p. 81.

155 Abu al-Hai Lucknawi, op. cit., p. 173.

156 Haji Khalifah, op. cit., vol. III, p. 85.

pertaining to the hunting and slaughtering of the animals.[157]

Sharah Abyat al-Mufasal

This pamphlet is based on the rules of the Arabic poetry.[158]

Takmilat al-Sihah

This book is a valuable commentary as well as gist of some of the themes mentioned in six authentic books of *hadith*.[159]

'Ali bin Abu Bakr Marghinani

The celebrated jurist 'Ali bin Abu Bakr Marghinani is among the lofty figures of Mawara al-Nahr (Transoxiania) has ever produced. In the science of *usul al-fiqh* (methodology of Islamic jurisprudence) he is considered as the master architect who compiled major treatises to explore further advance in this field. 'Ali bin Abu Bakr Marghinani has extremely a dynamic stature into the various disciplines of the Islamic learning and is credited with the brilliant contribution done in the field of Islamic jurisprudence. The science of Islamic jurisprudence remained his focal concern in which he compiled such a great share that nobody among his contemporaries as well as among the jurists proceeding in the forthcoming generations could think of. The grand jurist, al-Marghinani was born in Marghinan (vicinity in nowadays Uzbekistan) in AH 511/CE 1114, at the time when Islamic society and culture had moved far ahead from the rudimentary phase. Marghinani, as is reported by his biographer, al-Qarshi, travelled to almost all the centres of Islamic learning in Mawara al-Nahr, Arab and Iraq and equipped himself with the latest trends and understanding of the confronting issues in Islamic

---

[157] Gangohi, op. cit., p. 559.

[158] Ibid., p. 560.

[159] Haji Khalifah, op. cit., vol. III, p. 87.

jurisprudence. He gained expertise in various disciplines of Islamic knowledge and distinguished himself as an illustrious jurist capable of understanding the paramount link adjoining society and religion. With this inevitable distinction Marghinani could manifest the relation between the time and the text helping him to explore several socio-legal issues prevailed during his time. The contemporary sources, as it is recorded, mention him as the most pervasive figure that surpassed his teachers and contemporaries with such distinction. Consequently, the famous biographer, al-Qarshi holds:

اقر له أهل مصره بالفضل و التقدم

> His contemporaries acknowledge him with pride and honour (due to his expertise and scholarship).[160]

The reputed jurist, 'Ali bin Abu Bakr Marghinani compiled his travelogue entitled *Mujam al-Shuyukh* which narrates his great efforts to travel to far-off and distant locations of the then Muslim world. The famous Orientalists, P.M. Holt and E.J. Brill, in their celebrated work *Encyclopaedia of Islam* (Leiden, 1953) makes description of his acquisition of knowledge in these words:

> The author of celebrated Hidayah, 'Ali bin Abu Bakr Marghinani acquired his knowledge on his travels, then still the usual way of studying Islam.[161]

'Ali bin Abu Bakr Marghinani gained expertise in diverse branches of Islamic learning and devoted himself exclusively to the study of Islamic jurisprudence. He has been a born jurist, who could properly interpret and utilize, through his brilliance,

[160] Al-Qarshi, op. cit., vol. I, p. 13.

[161] *Encyclopaedia of Islam*, vol. IV, p. 558.

both the text and reason for socio-legal deductions. He justified a clear understanding of the legal text and its application through approved instruments of *qiyas* (analogy) and *istehsan* (public good).[162] Making account of his multi-dimensional character in the field of Islamic jurisprudence, Al-Qarshi holds:

> 'Ali bin Abu Bakr Marghinani was an extraordinary luminary, jurist, *hafiz*, traditionist and exegist, having command in different spheres of learning. He has been an outstanding scholar and champion of literature. Eyes never witnessed anybody like him.[163]

The anecdotes and record of his travels are evident to the fact that he associated himself with the much reliable sources both texual as well as human available at that time. This passion kept the tradition of jurisprudence alive and encompassing. To a great extent he remained busy, throughout his life for the compilation of an authoritative literature in the field of Islamic jurisprudence. Absolutely it was this concern that during his stay in Samarkand, al-Marghinani remained in the circle of Qays bin Ishaq (d. AH 527) who was an ultimate authority in teaching jurisprudence and its related fields. Moreover, the two great figures associated with the field of teaching law in Mawara al-Nahr, Ahmad bin 'Umar Nasafi (d. AH 552) and Asbhijabi (d. AH 535), both from Samarkand held him with great esteem and licensed him for the transmission of juristic tradition to the forthcoming generations. These reputed figures have done a marvellous contribution to Islamic jurisprudence.[164] Similarly, in the city of Neshapur, al-Marghinani benefited from 'Abdullah bin Muhammad Sa'di (d. AH 547) who was a dynamic figure in teaching jurisprudence and its principles.[165]

---

162 *Encyclopaedia of Islam*, vol. IV, p. 557.

163 Al-Qarshi, op. cit., vol. II, p. 345.

164 Ibid., p. 52.

165 Ibid., p. 249.

'Ali bin Abu Bakr Marghinani remained vibrant throughout his entire career. He visited Merv and benefited from Muhammad bin Abu Bakr, a great traditionist and jurist. Sheikh Muhammad bin Husayn who narrated *Sahih al-Muslim* also added to the experiences of al-Marghinani. Sheikh Muhammad bin Hassan and Muhammad bin 'Abd al-Rahman Maruzi were among his reliable sources for the study of *hadith* during his stay in Merv.[166] Al-Marghinani remained in Balkh for two years and during this stay he benefited from Sa'id bin Yusuf al-Hanafi, 'Umar bin Muhammad Bistami and Muhammad bin Muhammad al-Hanafi who acquainted him with the science of *hadith* and its role in the Islamic legal theory.[167]

'Ali bin Abu Bakr al-Marghinani's stay in Bukhara was a crucial and turning point. Indeed it is in this city where he attained knowledge from the dynamic jurists like 'Umar bin 'Abd al-'Aziz bin Mazah (d. AH 536) who compiled books on jurisprudence and *'ilm-al usul*, Ahmad bin 'Abd al-'Aziz, Muhammad bin 'Abd al-Rehman Bukhari (d. AH 546), 'Uthman bin 'Ali Baqandi and al-Tarazi (d. AH 570). These great figures, as holds al-Qarshi, influenced him and remained his source of inspiration.[168]

In the city of Marghinan, 'Ali bin Abu Bakr al-Marghinani approached the experts of various academic fields to receive all what he could attain from them. He had a keen insight to bring the science of *hadith* and *fiqh* much closer and identical to each other. In this regard, it is reported that he travelled to the scholars that included 'Abdullah bin Abu al-Fath and Sa'id bin Asad who for the first time, made him acquainted with the legal dimensions and trends in *hadith*.[169]

After the compilation of different courses in Mawara al-

---

[166] Al-Qarshi, op. cit., vol. II, p. 249.

[167] Ibid., vol. III, p. 391.

[168] Ibid., p. 57.

[169] Ibid., vol. I, p. 246.

Nahr, he visited Baghdad and learned *hadith* from 'Ali bin Hassan Ghaznvi, a scholar *par excellence* in his respective field. In AH 544, al-Marghinani visited Mecca, Madina and other cities of Hejaz to gain expertise in teaching and narrating *Sihah al-Sittah* (six cannonical treatises of *hadith*).[170]

The grand jurist and scholar *par excellence*, Zahir al-Din bin Ilyas (d. AH 547) was a dynamic and reputed figure in the field of Islamic jurisprudence. He was a famous disciple of Imam Bazudi (d. AH 482). Al-Marghinani benefited from him for a long period and this association has been mentioned in these couplets:

إسعد فقد لقيت أفضل با لناس ابى المعانى زياد بن الياس
و انزل بناديه تلقى المجد مبتسما الأفضل فى نفحات الورد و الآ س
و الز به من زمان جائر نكد فما يخرج الليا لى عنده آس
إن لم تحط بهداه فى فضائله فقصد بالشي بيدى بالمقياس
جواد البرامك فو نطق بنى ساعده فى حكم احنف فى فضل بنى عباس

> Run as you have met bestowed among the people, Ziyad bin Ilyas. Remain and stay with him you will attain dignity and honour. Seek his shelter as he will make you safe. If you fail to understand his highness, even then he is the best example to be followed. He is as kind as the Bermikides, eloquent as Bani Sa'ad, just as Ahnaf and vigorous as Ibn Abas.[171]

Ibn Kamal Pasha (d. AH 940), a great jurist, author and biographer, holds that al-Marghinani was really the pride of his age who is credited with the *magnum opus al-Hidayah*, a treatise ever authored in the history of Islamic jurisprudence.[172] Ibn Kamal Pasha classifies the Islamic legal experts into several

---

170 Al-Qarshi, op. cit., vol. II, p. 53.

171 Ibid., vol. I, p. 246.

172 Ibn Kamal Pasha, *Risalat al-Waqf*, Cairo, 1952, p. 9.

categories as per their legal stature. In this classification he mentions al-Marghinani in *al-Tabqa al-Khamisah* (fifth category) of the Hanafi jurists technically known as *ashab al-tarjih*, a category consisting of the most distinguished jurists who compared and analysed various legal deductions and chose a better and preferable deduction to suit the circumstances.[173] While performing this exercise, the legal superiority of a particular school of thought is admired that resolves or deduces for an existing legal problem:

> و الطبقة الخامسة من أصحاب الترجيح من المقلدين ،كأبى الحسن أحمد القدورى و الشيخ الإسلام برهان الدين على بن أبى بكر المرغينانى و أمثالهم و شأنهم تفضيل الروايات على بعض بقولهم هذا أولى ،هذا أصح ،هذا أوضح ،و هذا أوفق بالقياس ،هذا أوفق بالناس

> And fifth category (of the jurists) comprises of the jurists like al-Qudoori and al-Marghinani whose expertise is to look into the nature of narrations/interpretations as which one is preferable and which is not, i.e. which is valid, open, nearer to any valid deduction or beneficial to people.[174]

Among the contemporaries of 'Ali bin Abu Bakr al-Marghinani, we can mention the author of *al-Badayah wa Sanayah*, Fakhr al-din Qazi Khan, the author of *al-Fatawah*, Ibrahim bin Mansur, the commentrator of *al-Mazhab* and Ibn Rushd (d. AH 595), the author of *Bidayat al-Mujtahid*.[175] His contemporaries and disciples also include Abu Bakr bin Mas'ud Kasani (d. AH 587) the author of *al-Sanayah*, 'Abd al-Satar Kardari, Mahmud Asturwashni, 'Umar bin Mahmud, Muhammad bin 'Ali Samarqandi, Fakhr al-din, Kuhistani and Zarnuji, the author of *Talim al-Muta'alim*.[176]

---

173 Al-Qarshi, op. cit., vol. I, p. 246.

174 Abu al-Hai Lucknawi, op. cit., p. 57.

175 Haji Khalifah, op. cit., vol. II, p. 1821.

176 Ibid., vol. IV, p. 1830.

During the last years of his life he restricted himself from travelling to far-off distances and remained in Samarkand till his death in AH 593/CE 1196. He left behind him a band of reputed disciples and a wide range of compilations, an ample proof of his expertise in different branches of Islamic learning.[177]

CONTRIBUTION

'Ali bin Abu Bakr Marghinani has to his credit a number of reputed treatises compiled in various branches of Islamic knowledge. His prolific carrier conform keen insight into diverse branches of learning which is evident through his biographic sketch by al-Qarshi.[178] He is reported to have mastered in almost all the branches of Islamic learning; however confined himself within the course of Islamic jurisprudence due to its socio-legal character. Al-Marghinani, being a prolific jurist, wrote exclusively on Islamic jurisprudence and it is this particular field to which he contributed the following rare treatises:

Nashr al-Mazahib

Nashr al-Mazahib is a monumental work in the field of Islamic jurisprudence. Al-Marghinani, in this work, makes a critical study of the different schools of jurisprudence and analyses their approach regarding the deduction of juristic verdicts.[179]

Manasik al-Hajj

Manasik al-Hajj was compiled to facilitate and comment upon the basic verdicts pertaining to this obligation. The etiquettes of *Hajj* and its related issues have been discussed in a thorough manner.[180]

---

177 Haji Khalifah, op. cit., vol. II, p. 1821.

178 Ibid., p. 1830.

179 Ibid., p. 1201.

180 Ibid., vol. I, p. 660.

Al-Faraiz al-'Uthmani

Al-Faraiz al-'Uthmani is a treatise compiled to resolve the issues concerning the law of inheritance.[181]

Al-Mazid fi Furu al-Hanafiyah

The work *Al-Mazid fi Furu al-Hanafiyah* is a treatise examining the nature and scope of the narrations deployed in the Hanafi School of Law. It debates upon the legal instruments derived for the deduction of rulings from the primary sources of law.[182]

Mukhtarat al-Fatawa

Al-Marghinani compiled this work to put forth various dimensions of a legal interpretation and insight of the earlier jurists to review and interpret their decrees and methods for resolution of the socio-legal issues. As such, the work is a record of the decrees issued by the celebrated jurists of the Hanafi School of Law regarding the resolution of the socio-legal issues.[183]

Mukhtarat al-Nawazil

This treatise is a collection of the narrations upon which the Hanafi scholars have relied upon and conformed their distinction and viewpoint. Al-Marghinani authored this book to relate the significance of the Hanafi methodology and its comprehensive legal character for the process of legal extraction.[184]

Al-Muntaqa al-Marfu

This book is also in the field of Islamic jurisprudence and carries legal deductions from *ahadith* which have authentic as well as reliable sources besides the concise chain of narrators.[185]

---

181 Haji Khalifah, op. cit., vol. II, p. 1626.

182 Ibid., p. 1622.

183 Ibid., vol. III, p. 2032.

184 'Ali bin Abu Bakr Marghinani, *Al-Hidayah*, Delhi, 1994, vol. I, p. 3.

185 Ibid.

Kitab al-Tajnis wa al-Mazid

The work *Kitab al-Tajnis wa al-Mazid* has been authored by al-Marghinani during his stay in Samarkand. The work is a reliable masterpiece and is a collection of the decrees issued by the scholars of Bukhara, Rushdan, Merv and Marghinan.[186]

Kitab al-Hidayah Sharah Bidayat al-Mubtadi

This monumental work is considered to be the most incredible contribution to the field of Islamic jurisprudence. This masterpiece speaks of the ripe scholarship and virtuous expertise of al-Marghinani as a renowned theorist and legal expert. The reputed historian and biographer Haji Khalifa praises this *magnum opus* in these lines:

إن الهداية كالقرآن قد نسخت ما صنعوا قبلها فى الشرع من كتب

فاحفظوا قواعدها و اسلكوا مسالكها يسلم مقالك من زيغ و من كذب

> Verily *al-Hidayah* can be compared to Quran, which has abrogated the early gospels. So did *al-Hidayah* (it overshaded early juristic literature). Its parallel has never been authored. So try to understand its rules and context, follow its path; it will keep you away from undue and false judgements.[187]

Al-Marghinani's son, Imad al-Din a renowned scholar and jurist who taught this treatise for years together and remained associated with it since its compilation, holds:

كتاب الهداية يهدى إلى الهدى إلى حافظه و يجلو ا العمى

فلازمه و احفظه يا ذا الجبى فمن ناله نال أقصى المنى

---

[186] Charles Hamilton, *Hidayah* (Eng. tr.), Delhi, 1994, pp. xiv-xv.

[187] Haji Khalifah, op. cit., vol. III, p. 2032.

> *Al-Hidayah* guides its learners and takes away darkness (ignorance) from them. O the intelligent, just hold it and learn it. Whosoever attained it, verily, got the ever reached pinnacle in this world.[188]

Al-Marghinani began this profound juristic project in about AH 573 and completed it in thirteen consecutive years in AH 586. The treatise consists of fifty-seven books (*kitabs*) compiled on different religious, social, commercial, constitutional, criminal and judicial aspects of Islam. It is due to its legal practicability, authencity and socio-political relevance that the famous orientalist Charles Hamilton, the counsellor of first Governor-General of India, Warren Hastings (CE 1771-75), writes:

> I might be allowed to express a hope upon the subject, it is that, its future beneficial effects, in facilitating, the administration of justice throughout our Asiatic territories and uniting us still more with our Mussalman subjects.[189]

Al-Hidayah being a celebrated work in the field of Islamic jurisprudence has always been within the course of academic institutions at higher level and is still considered to be the authentic and reliable work pertaining to Muslim Personal Law. Charles Hamilton translated this treatise into English with the same purpose and added explanatory notes to make an illustrious explanation of its socio-legal content. This celebrated work had already caught the attention of Muslim legal experts who wrote extensive cannotations to it. Visualizing the socio-legal implications of *al-Hidayah*, Muslim jurists, explored its contents, methodology and explanation, and added valuable commentaries to be utilized for the proper understanding of the law.[190]

---

188 Haji Khalifah, op. cit., vol. III, p. 2037.

189 Charles Hamilton, op. cit., 1994, pp. xiv-xv.

190 Ibid.

Commentaries on al-Hidayah

Al-Fawaid: It is considered to be the first commentary on *al-Hidayah*. This commentary was written by Qazi Hamid al-Din Bukhari (d. AH 627).[191]

Nihayat al-Kifayah: This commentary is the juristic venture of Taj al-Shari'ah 'Umar bin Sadr (d. AH 272).[192]

Al-Inayah: This commentary on *al-Hidayah* was written by Ahmad bin Ibrahim (d. AH 710) and later on explanatory and additional notes were prepared by Sa'ad din Ahmad (d. AH 862).[193]

Al-Nihayah: This commentary on *al-Hidayah* was compiled by Hisam al-din Husayn bin 'Ali (d. AH 610) and was annotated by Mahmud al-Qunavi (d. AH 770) under the title *Al-Khulasah fi Fawaid al-Hidayah*.[194]

Miraj al-Dirayah: This commentary was written by Muhammad bin Muhammad al-Bukhari (d. AH 745).[195]

Gayat al-Bayan wa Nadirat al-Aqran: This commentary was written by Amir Katib bin Amir 'Umar (d. AH 758). It is a valuable addition to Islamic jurisprudence. This commentary is in three volumes and was completed in twenty-six years.[196]

Al-Kifayah: This work is a scholarly venture of Jalal al-din Karlani (d. AH 767).[197]

Sharah al-Hidayah: This commentary was written by 'Abdullah bin Ahmad Nasafi (d. AH 715). The reputed scholar is reported to have completed this work in Baghdad in AH 700.[198]

---

191 Haji Khalifah, op. cit., vol. III, p. 2037.

192 Ibid.

193 Ibid., p. 2038.

194 Ibid., p. 2039.

195 Ibn Humam, *Fath al-Qadeer*, Beirut, 1997, vol. II, p. 163.

196 Haji Khalifah, op. cit., vol. III, p. 2033.

197 Ibid., p. 2036.

198 Ibid., p. 2037.

Fatah al-Qadeer: Among the commentaries on *al-Hidayah, Fatah al-Qadeer* is considered to be the most reliable, logical and illustrious compilation authored in the field of Islamic jurisprudence. This work was compiled by Muhammad bin 'Abd al-Wahid Ibn Humam (d. AH 841). The towering scholar and intellectual of fourteenth century CE, Shei<u>kh</u> 'Abd al-Haq Muhadith Dehlavi, affirms his contribution to the discipline of Islamic jurisprudence and makes a scholarly remark regarding Ibn Humam's *Fatah al-Qadeer*:

شرح هداية از شيخ ابن همام جزاه الله خير الجزاء تلافى آن نموده و تحقيق كار فرموده است .

> Ibn Humam, may Allah bestow him the pre-eminent mercy, has done a great job by means of intense care and investigation (while making commentary on *al-Hidayah*).[199]

This commentary on *al-Hidayah* was published from Beirut, Lebanon, in 1997 in two volumes.[200]

Nataij al-Afkar fi Kashf al-Rumuz wa al-Asrar: This commentary on *al-Hidayah* was compiled by Qazi Zadah (d. AH 988) and is a magnificent work in the field of Islamic jurisprudence.[201]

Al-Tawsheeh: It is also a valuable commentary written by 'Umar bin Ishaq al-Ghaznavi (d. AH 773).[202]

Sharah al-Hidayah: It was compiled by 'Alauddin 'Ali bin Muhammad <u>Kh</u>alati (d. AH 707). This commentary on *al-Hidayah* is in two volumes.[203]

Al-'Inayah: A reputed commentary on *al-Hidayah* written by Akmal din Muhammad Babarti (d. AH 786), it was annotated

---

[199] Haji Khalifah, op. cit., vol. III, p. 2036.

[200] Ibid., p. 2041.

[201] Ibid., p. 2039.

[202] Ibid., p. 2040.

[203] Ibid., p. 2042.

by Muhammad bin Ibrahim al-Misri (d. AH 1066) and is in two volumes.[204]

Sharah al-Hidayah: *Sharah al-Hidayah* was compiled by 'Ali bin 'Uthman Turkamni (d. AH 750). After his sudden death, some necessary notes and explanations were added by his son Jamal al-din 'Abdullah (d. AH 769).[205]

Al-Binayah: It is a renowned commentary on *al-Hidayah* written by Qazi Badr al-din 'Aini (d. AH 755).[206]

Nihayah al-Nihayah: *Nihayah al-Nihayah* was written by Muhammad bin Mahmud (d. AH 790).[207]

Sharah: This commentary was compiled by Ahmad bin Hassan Tabrazi (d. AH 746).[208]

Sharah: This commentary was written by Ahmad bin 'Uthman Marini (d. AH 745).[209]

Sharah al-Hidayah: It was written by Sanan al-din Yusuf al-Rumi (d. AH 1018). After his death, necessary additions and notes were added by Muhammad bin Mustafa (d. AH 1039).[210]

Irshad al-Dirayah: This commentary was compiled by Mustafa bin Zakariya Kirmani (d. AH 809). It is also a reputed addition in the field of Islamic jurisprudence.[211]

Sharah al-Hidayah: This commentary on *al-Hidayah* was compiled by Shiekh 'Ali (d. AH 775).[212]

---

204 Haji Khalifah, op. cit., vol. III, p. 2045.

205 *Dairah al-Ma'arif*, op. cit., vol. 20, p. 466.

206 Ibid., p. 462.

207 Ibid., p. 465.

208 Ibid., p. 466.

209 Ibid., p. 467.

210 Haji Khalifah, op. cit., vol. III, p. 2039.

211 *Dairah al-Ma'arif*, op. cit., vol. 20, p. 466.

212 Ibid., p. 462.

Sharah: It was written by al-Khadad Dehlavi (d. AH 1026).[213]

Sharah al-Hidayah: This commentary on *al-Hidayah* was written by Shams al-din Muhammad bin 'Uthman al-Hariri (d. AH 767).[214]

Zubdat al-Dirayah: Qazi 'Abd al-Rahim Amadi (d. AH 923) compiled it.[215]

Sharah al-Hidayah: This commentary on *al-Hidayah* was written by Ibrahim bin 'Ali al-Damshaqi (d. AH 744).[216]

Sharah al-Hidayah: A valuable addition to the commentaries of *al-Hidayah,* it was written by Ahmad bin Hassan al-Zarkashi (d. AH 738).[217]

Sharah al-Hidayah: It was written by Taj al-din Ahmad bin 'Abd al-Qadir (d. AH 749).[218]

Sharah al-Hidayah: This commentary on *al-Hidayah* was compiled by Sa'ad al-Din Taftazani (d. AH 906).[219]

Sharah al-Hidayah: It was written by Najm al-Din Ishaq bin 'Ali (d. AH 711).[220]

Sharah al-Hidayah: This commentary on *Hidayah* was written by Syed Sharief al-Jurjani (d. AH 816).[221]

Al-Dirayah: This was written by Abu 'Abdullah Muhammad bin Mubarak (d. AH 918).[222]

---

[213] *Dairah al-Ma'arif,* op. cit., vol. 20, p. 465.

[214] Ibid., p. 468.

[215] Ibid., p. 467.

[216] Gangohi, op. cit., p. 265.

[217] *Dairah al-Ma'arif,* op. cit., vol. 20, p. 466.

[218] Ibid., p. 465.

[219] Ibid.

[220] Ibid., p. 467.

[221] Ibid., p. 476.

[222] Gangohi, op. cit., p. 264.

Tawajih al-'Inayah li Majma Shuruh al-Wiqayah: This commentary on *al-Hidayah* is a valuable addition to Islamic jurisprudence. It was compiled by Muhammad bin al-Muhib (d. AH 838) in two volumes.[223]

Sharah al-Hidiyah: It was written by Taqi al-din Abu Bakr (d. AH 829).[224]

Sharah al-Hidayah: This five-volume commentary was written by Najm al-din Ibrahim al-Tartusi (d. AH 757).[225]

Rauzat al-Akhyar: It was compiled by an unknown scholar whose biographical account has not been mentioned.[226]

Sharah al-Hidayah: This work was compiled by Hamid al-din Mukhlis bin Abdullah al-Hindi. Unfortunately this commentary remained incomplete due to his long illness.[227]

Gayat al-Si'ayah fi Hil ma fi al-Hidayah: This commentary on *al-Hidayah* was compiled by Muhammad Hanif Gangohi. The second part of this commentary — *Talu al-Niyarain* — is in Urdu.[228]

Ashraf al-Hidayah: This commentary on *al-Hidayah* was written by Maulana Jameel Ahmad Sukhrudvi. It is in eight volumes and was published from Deoband (India) in 1984. The language of this commentary is Urdu.[229]

Ashraf al-Hidayah: This commentary was written by Mufti Muhammad Yusuf and was published from Deoband (India) in 1992. The language of this commentary is Urdu.[230]

---

223 Jameel Ahmad, *Ashraf al-Hidayah*, Deoband, India, 1984, p. 18.

224 Haji Khalifah, op. cit., vol. III, p. 2034.

225 Ibid., p. 2036.

226 Ibid., p. 2030.

227 *Ma'arif*, op. cit., vol. 20, p. 345.

228 Haji Khalifah, op. cit., vol. III, p. 2034.

229 *Ma'arif*, vol. 20, 1984, p. 347.

230 Ibn Humam, op. cit., vol. II, p. 87.

In addition to these works and commentaries on *al-Hidayah*, some traditionists and reputed scholars have worked with their utmost capacities to investigate into the material, its nature, and sources of the *ahadith* mentioned in *al-Hidayah*. Al-Marghinani, the celebrated author of *al-Hidayah*, while compiling this monumental work, relied upon his predecessors, as being the prolific style that time, and did not trace the references while narrating deductions from *ahadith*. Hence, the following works have been compiled to trace the references of the material explored in *al-Hidayah*:

Al-Inayah bi Ma'rifat al-Ahadith al-Hidayah: This celebrated work was compiled by Sheikh 'Abd al-Qadir al-Qarshi (d. AH 775), the renowned disciple of al-Marghinani.[231]

Al-Kifayah fi Ma'rifat al-Ahadith al-Hidayah: This reputed work is the result of the efforts and ripe scholarship of Shiekh 'Alauddin 'Ali bin 'Uthman al-Turkamani (d. AH 750).[232]

Nasb al-Rayah li Ahadith al-Hidayah: This treatise was compiled by Shiekh Jamal al-din 'Abdullah bin Yusuf al-Zayl'i (d. AH 762).[233]

Muniyat al-'Ama fi ma Fata min Takhrij al-Hidayah: This reputed work was compiled by Shiekh Qasim bin Qatlubigah and was published by 'Allama Zahid Kausari al-Misri in CE 1950.[234]

Al-Dirayah fi Muntakhib Ahadith al-Hidayah: It was compiled by Shiekh Ahmad bin 'Ali bin Hajr al-Asqalani (d. AH 852).[235]

---

231 Ibn Humam, op. cit., vol. II, p. 88.

232 'Ali bin Abu Bakr Marghinani, op. cit., vol. I, p. 118.

233 Ibn Humam, vol. II, p. 91.

234 Haji Khalifah, op. cit., vol. III, p. 2035.

235 Gangohi, op. cit., p. 265.

5

Prolific Centres of Islamic Jurisprudence

THE geographical region, Mawara al-Nahr (Transoxania) or what now is Central Asia has been among the heartlands of the Islamic civilization that carried on the spirit of Islamic tradition for centuries together. It is from this particular region that Islam moved to various directions making the message of the revealed faith universal and utilitarian. This vast region entered the realm of Islam around CE 715 during the reign of the Umayyads (CE 661–751) and contributed an immense share to the Islamic civilization by virtue of discovering and exploring certain aspects of Islamic sciences as well as adding glamour to socio-political and academic persuits. The emergence of the Muslim legacy in Central Asia is result of the intellectual process initiated by a number of intellectuals, caliphs, Amirs and the men of letters who established reputed institutions and associated themselves with this literary convention. To enhance this cerebral persuit a number of efforts were underway both on social as well on the political level to achieve the ultimate intellectual benefits. The world history in general and Central Asian in particular is evident to the fact that the vast territory of the steppe was at centre of the rich cultured, religious and commercial developments that occurred here over a period of two millennia. Especially along the axis defined by the Silk Route (Shariah-i-Abreshim) between Europe and China, included in present-day Uzbekistan, were the three chief silk-route outposts of Bukhara, Khiva and Samarkand. The Central Asia, especially the cities of medieval Uzbekistan, as depicted in the chronicles, had established strong religious and cultural ties with Arab, Iraq and Persia and had remained a hub of Muslim legacy that flourished here during ninth and tenth centuries CE/the second and third centuries of Islamic era.[1]

The cities of Central Asia shared a great past with the Islamic caliphate and also retained the Muslim legacy for centuries together. Andijon, city and administrative centre in nowadays far eastern Uzbekistan in Andijon province, is at the south-eastern edge of the Farghana Valley. It has remained a centre of Islamic academia especially during the Samanid rule. Andijon is about 475 km east of Tashqand, and about 45 km west of Osh, Kyrgyzstan. Andijon is a centre for oil production and has a few oil refineries. Cotton growing and processing are the dominant economic activities that regulate the per capita and Gross National Product (GNP). Andijon sits on an ancient riverbed (Say River) and is known to have existed since the ninth century on a trade route into western China. Andijon was the fifteenth-century capital of the Farghana Valley, and in the eighteenth and ninteenth-centuries a part of the Khokand Khanate centred in the present-day Quqon. In 1876, Andijon was captured by Russian forces and annexed to the Soviet Federation. After the disintegration of the Union of Soviet Socialist Republics (USSR) in 1991, Andijon is a part of the Uzbek territory and is famous for the tomb of the Umayyad general Qutaybah bin Muslim who conquered Mawara al-Nahr during CE 712-15.[2]

---

1 Sayyuti, *Tarikh al-Khulafa*, Deoband, 1989, p. 107.

2 H.A.R. Gibb, *The Arab Conquests in Central Asia*, New York, 1970, p. 39.

The Farghana Valley's last local Muslim struggle against the rule of the Russian Tsar took place at Andijon in CE 1898 which opened a new phase of political discourse. This being an attempt to overthrow the Czarist occupation was dealt with extreme tyrany and Muslim of this region had to carve their space into their own domain. The well-known Babur Literary Museum is also in Andijon. It is named after Zahiruddin Muhammad Babur, who was born in Andijon in CE 1483 and founded the Mughal Empire of northern India in CE 1526. The museum was opened in 1989 on the site of his residence in celebration of the 460th year of publication of his autobiography entitled *Baburnamah*, published in English as the *Memories of Babur*.[3]

The Bukhara city, western Uzbekistan, capital of Bukhara *Wilayat* (region), is located in an oasis on the Zeravshan River. The city is situated in a region producing natural gas, cotton, fruit and silk. It has industries manufacturing textiles, processed Karakul pelt, carpets and clothing. Among Bukhara's many architectural monuments, some dating from the ninth century CE, are several mosques, the Ark Fortress (now a museum) and the mausoleum of Amir Isma'il Samani (tenth century). Founded during the first century CE, Bukhara was an important trade and cultural centre when it was conquered in early eighth century by the Muslims. It became a leading centre of Islamic learning under the Arabs and the Persian Samanid dynasty, which held the city and the adjacent provinces from ninth to tenth century. The city also remained a significant centre for socio-religious and political activities by the time of Qarakhanids and Tatars. In the sixteenth century CE, it became the capital of an Uzbek Khanate, and in the eighteenth century became an Emirate. The Emirate was captured in 1866 by Russia, which held it as a protectorate from 1868–1920. With the Russian

---

[3] *Encyclopaedia of Islam*, ed. E.J. Brill, Leiden, 1953, vol. V, p. 1122.

invasion, the Amir was removed, and the city was made the capital of the Bukharan People's Soviet Republic. Bukhara, a meritorious centre of Islamic civilization, was incorporated into the Uzbek Soviet Socialist Republic; in 1924. With the dissolution of the Russian Federation in 1991, Bukhara nowadays is a part of Uzbekistan and is still considered to be among the meritorious cities of Islam.[4]

The Farghana city is also among the pearls of Islam. It is in eastern Uzbekistan, located at the southern edge of the Farghana Valley. Farghana is about 420 km east of Tashqand, the capital of Uzbekistan, and about 75 km west of Andijon. Farghana has been a centre for oil production in the Farghana Valley since the region's first oil refinery was built near the city in 1908. Since then more refineries have been added and Farghana is one of the most important centres of oil production and refining in Uzbekistan. Natural gas from western Uzbekistan is transported by pipeline to the Valley, where it is used to produce fertilizer for this developing country. The Farghana Valley was the most important irrigated cotton region of the former USSR. Cotton growing and processing was the dominant economic activity here for centuries and the Muslims of this region were having unparrelleled expertise in this industry besides their taste for intellectual and artistic activities. The city has a unbroken chain of water-channels that supply water from small streams flowing from the surrounding mountains. The great Farghana Canal, built almost entirely by hand during the 1930, passes through the northern part of the city. Farghana was founded as a garrison town by the Russians after they captured the Khanate of Khokand. The city contains memories of the Islamic tradition and is part of the present-day Uzbekistan.[5]

---

[4] Gibb, op. cit., p. 42.

[5] Ibid., p. 41.

Tashqand city has also remained a magnificent centre of Muslim legacy in Central Asia. The city is in eastern Uzbekistan and is the capital of the country as well as of the Tashqand *wilayat*. It is located in an Oasis near the Chirchiq River, a cotton- and fruit-growing region. Tashqand is a major industrial and transportation centre and is also known for world-famous academic institutions. It has industries producing machineries, cotton and silk textiles, chemicals, tobacco products, and furniture. As a centre of Uzbek culture, Tashqand has several large libraries and is the seat of the Uzbek Academy of Sciences and numerous other institutions of higher learning. The first mention of Tashqand dates from the seventh century CE, although it was probably founded in the first century BCE. The city was conquered, successively, by the Arab Muslims in the eighth century CE, by Genghis Khan in the early thirteenth century, and by Amir Timur in the fourteenth century. It was annexed by Russia in CE 1865, and the new Russian city was built around the older town. Tashqand succeeded Samarkand as the capital of the Uzbek Soviet Socialist Republic of the Soviet Union in 1930. With the disintegration of USSR, Tashqand became the capital of independent Uzbekistan in 1991.[6]

The world-famous city of Samarkand has deep roots with the Islamic tradition and has been mentioned in the Muslim chronicles among the foremost territories that entered the manifold of Islam during CE 715. The city is situated in central Uzbekistan and is located in the irrigated valley of the Zeravshan River; the city has industries that produce tea, textiles, fertilizers and motor-vehicle parts. It is the oldest city in Central Asia and is divided into a newly-built section and an old quarter that has, among other monuments, mosques built during the ninth–fifteenth centuries. The city also

[6] Masud al-Hassan, *History of Islam*, Delhi, 2006, vol. 1, pp. 168-69.

contains the fifteenth-century mausoleum of the Turkic conqueror Amir Timur. Nowadays, the city is the seat of a university, a museum of ancient history and has an efficient linkage with the Islamic academic and religious ethos rooted since centuries.[7]

The site of Samarkand was settled about 2000 BCE. It was the capital of Sogdiana, an ancient Persian province. It subsequently grew as a trade centre on the route between China and the mediterranean region bridging the gap among different cultures. During the early eighth century CE, it was conquered by the Arab Muslims and soon became a crucial centre of Islamic culture. In CE 1220, Samarkand was almost completely destroyed by the Mongol tribals led by Genghis Khan. It flourished again when Amir Timur made it the capital of his empire in CE 1367. The empire declined in the fifteenth century, and Samarkand was taken in CE 1500 by the Uzbeks. In CE 1784, the city was conquered by the Emirate of Bukhara and in CE 1868, it was captured by Russia. From 1924-30, Samarkand remained the capital of the Uzbek Soviet Socialist Republic and was an important garrison for Russian troops.[8] Finally with the dissolution of the USSR, the city got included within the territory of Uzbekistan.

The cities of the Central Asia mentioned here hold oldest and most imperative cultures of the world heritage over a period of two millennia. The religion of Islam had been a vital socio-cultural force that shaped the ethos of steppe people from eighth century onwards. The emergence of Islamic civilization revolutionized almost all the spheres of life and contributed an immense share to develop its relation with the central authority of the Muslim caliphate from the time of the

---

[7] *Encyclopaedia of Islam*, p. 1122.

[8] Abad Shahpuri, *Rus mein Musalman Qumayn*, Delhi, 1991, pp. 208-09.

Umayyads. Its role of contributing to socio-religious dynamism cannot be overlooked. Islam's cultural, religious and civilizational aspects have turned this region to a meritorious land that produced as well as retained the identity of Muslims even during the crucial times. The reputed scholars who regulated the Islamic tradition of this region undoubtedly have contributed a lot to the development of Islamic religious and social sciences especially till the end of the Abbasid period (CE 750–1258). It was during the rule of major local sundry dynasties that a series of magnificent academic institutions got established and aspirants even from the far-off distances came here for the persuit of excellence.[9]

Reputed Centres of Academic Excellence of Medieval Central Asia (8th–15th century CE)

The beginning of the Islamic intellectualism here dates back to the conquest of Mawara al-Nahr by the Umayyad general Qutaybah bin Muslim who annexed the steppe to the Muslim caliphate during CE 712-15. Simultaneously with the time of the Umayyad regime, the chief vicinities of Central Asia maintained their connection with the reputed academic centres of Baghdad, Basrah, Kufa, Damascus, Mecca and Medina for scholarly persuits. Regarding the prestigious centres of the Islamic caliphate that established and retained the academic tradition, Central Asian cities have played a vital role for the dissemination of Islamic sciences. Central Asia of the medieval times has been upright for the cultivation and nourishing spirit of the Islamic legacy for centuries together. Subsequently, it is this land to which the scholars from the far-off regions used to travel to study and attain the valuable and rare treatises on Islamic intellectualism.[10] From CE 715 onwards, *mualimin*

---

9 M. Tahir, *Islamic Institutions*, Delhi, 1998, p. 110.

10 W.M. Watt, *The Formative Period of Islamic Thought*, Edinburgh, 1973, p. 79.

(teachers) of Quran and *hadith* could be seen into the steppe involved in the propagation and teaching of the Islamic congregations. The local governors and *umal* (collectors) had to respond the socio-religious necessities so the men of letters were sent to the unruly people of the steppe for religious orientation.[11] In the reign of the Umayyad caliph Hisham (CE 724-43), a special class of scholars and students *ah al-'ilm* was deputed to this region to spread the knowledge of Islam throughout the conquered lands.[12] A renowned historian and prolific writer Jalaludin Sayyuti (CE 1445–1505) holds:

> They collected people around them and began to teach the most necessary principles and obligations to the common people to impart the knowledge of Islam.[13]

When the series of conquests in Mawara al-Nahr was going on, special attention was paid to the construction of mosques. Thus the mosque appeared as special centre for carrying the purpose of *da'wah wa al-irshad* (instruction and learning) as well as to teach the tenets of Quran and the Prophetic Sunnah. Simultaneously, the scholars and the students got associated with these centres and formed the starting point regarding the study and understanding of Quran and the Prophetic Sunnah.[14] Dahhak bin Muzahim (d. AH 105/CE 723), the exigist, traditionist and grammarian, had a *madrasa* in Kufa attended by 300 scholars and students, who are reported to have travelled to far-off places to spread the knowledge of Islam. A number of them are reported to have settled in Mawara al-Nahr to disseminate and publicize what they had attained from their learned predecessors.[15]

---

[11] W.M. Watt, *The Formative Period of Islamic Thought*, Edinburgh, 1973, p. 80.

[12] Khateeb Baghdadi, *Tarikh-i-Baghdad*, Lebanon, 1956, vol. I, p. 169.

[13] Ibid., p. 170.

[14] Masud al-Hassan, op. cit., vol. I, p. 172.

[15] Tahir, op. cit., p. 122.

In the reign of the Umayyad Caliph Al-Waleed (CE 705-15), his abled governor Qutaybah advanced against Balkh and Tukharistan. In CE 706 he marched to Bukhara and in CE 711 he crossed the Oxus conquering Khawarizm and Khiva.[16] In CE 712 Muslims conquered Samarkand and in CE 714 Qutaybah crossed Jaxartes and captured Farghana, Khojand and Shash.[17] Turkistan, Kashgar and Neshapur were annexed to the caliphate in the same year.[18] It was during the governorship of Qutaybah, that a number of mosques were constructed in the conquered territories of the Central Asia and special missions were carried out to promulgate Islamic teachings to the newly-conquered lands.[19]

The Umayyad Caliph Hisham, during his reign sent a number of missions to Mawara al-Nahr to invite the local population to the faith of Islam. Promises of reward (*talif al-qulub*) and remitting of poll-tax (*kharaj*) was guaranteed to the converts to the new faith.[20] These efforts as well as the missionary zeal of the Muslim scholars resulted in enormous conversions enabling Islam to root itself in this region. At this stage, the scholars, traditionists and jurists played a significant role by recruiting themselves and their disciples in the newly-annexed areas.[21] The scholars, who established themselves here, as it was a common practice, conferred their compilations and treatises for the public benefit which opened and nourished the intellectual and scholarly persuits in Central Asia. It was also a stride towards academic dynamism that Islam had brought to the world a century before with the proclamation

---

[16] Ibn Khalikan, *Wafiyat al-A'yan*, Beirut, 1977, vol. III, p. 182.

[17] Ibid., p. 182.

[18] Ibid., p. 183.

[19] Ibid., p. 185.

[20] Tahir, op. cit., p. 138.

[21] Sayyuti, op. cit., p. 109.

of the prophethood by Muhammad (SAW) in Arabia.[22]

Moreover, in addition to the grand mosques in Transoxania, there existed many instruction centres that imparted the general course of knowledge and study in various branches of Islamic education. We are told in the sources that *kutub khanas* (libraries) and *madrasas* (seminaries) played a vital role to retain the tradition of knowledge as well as to preserve it. A noted Muslim historian and intellectual, Khateeb Baghdadi has reported:

> Among other prominent centres of the academic excellence were *khizanat al-kutab* and *madrasas*. The *khazinat al-kutab* (libraries) was public, semi-public, private and some under state patronage. The semi-public libraries, often supplemented the libraries of the mosques, because they contained books in which the mosques were not much interested, notably on *mantiq* (logic), *falsafa*, geometry, astronomy, music, medicine and alchemy, the later were called *al-Ulum al-Qadima* or *al-Ulum al-Awail*. In this respect the academy Bayt al-Hikmah, founded by Mamun (AH 198–218/ CE 813-33) in Baghdad deserves first mention as his successors instructed to follow the same pattern in establishing academic centres throughout their jurisdictions.[23]

The academic institutions and prolific centres established during the Abbasid period (CE 750–1258) in Transoxania had been very much vibrant. Their approach to study the knowledge has also been prolific and accommodative. The Muslim academia, especially during this period studied diverse aspects of knowledge without separating or catagorizing them from one another. To them the tradition of knowledge was one; the ultimate goal of knowledge is the search for truth. Hence the scholars must deploy a variety of tools and

---

22 Sayyuti, op. cit., p. 110.

23 Tahir, op. cit., p. 142.

approaches to unveil and discover that truth. The contemporary academic terms such as inter-disciplinary, intra-disciplinary and multi-disciplinary or what is called scientific approach can be traced back to the Islamic prolification. The Muslim intellectuals interpreted the knowledge tradition in a much broader spectrum. The entire courses of study, in these reputed centres, were taught and studied with an equal consideration without separation of one from the other.[24]

The celebrated scholar and jurist, 'Ali bin Yehya (d. AH 275/CE 888) had a palace with a rich library to which the scholars and students of different parts of Transoxania used to travel for the search of excellent knowledge. The library was so highly equipped that the learners were able to study all branches of learning and was known as "Khizanah al-Hikmah" (the treasure of wisdom).[25]

In Mawsil, it is reported that Jafar bin Muhammad al-Mawsili (d. AH 323/CE 935), founded Dar al-'ilm (the house of knowledge) with a library adjacent to it where the scholars and students exclusively involved themselves with new researches. It is also reported that the scholars along their disciples worked together to improve the standard of higher academic activity in almost all branches of knowledge. The researchers and scholars were supplied with free paper in addition to the monthly grants. The founder of this institution used to deliver lectures on poetry and Arabic grammer. The intellectual offsprings from this centre flourished to distant regions of the Muslim caliphate including Mawara al-Nahr (Transoxiania) for the dissemination of the scholarly persuits.[26]

When the famous Muslim geographer, al-Maqdisi (CE 985) visited the institution founded by 'Adz al-Dawlah (AH 367-

---

[24] Sayyuti, op. cit., p. 111.

[25] Ibn Khalikan, op. cit., vol. III, p. 191.

[26] Haji Khalifah, *Kashf al-Zunun*, Istanbul, 1941, vol. III, p. 218.

72/CE 977-83), in Shiraz, he was astonished to see the high academic administration as well as care for the preservation of the knowledge tradition. He was overwhelmed and reported that the books were arranged in cases and listed in catalogues and the library was administrated by a director (*wakil*), an assistant (*khazin*) and an inspector (*mushrif*) who worked in a much disciplined and professional manner to serve both scholars as well as students.[27]

It was during the reign of the Abbasid Caliph al-Mamun (d. CE 833) that the intellectual activities throughout the caliphate received full attention and reached the pinnacle of academic heights. The scholastic centres throughout his caliphate had a uniform curriculam; the intellectuals of different disciplines worked in collaboration to promote the venture of knowledge. The caliph gave special instructions to jurists, traditionists and scholars to remain in touch with the central authority and to report for the resolution of the socio-political and economic issues. He ordered for the collection of valuable material on different aspects of knowledge and supplied it to the intellectual circles of his caliphate including some reputed centres of Transoxania. The *kutub khana* of Muhammad bin Husayn Baghdadi (d. CE 852) contained rare books, valuable manuscripts, ancient Persian and Greek writings, which were copied in abundance and sent to different parts of the caliphate including Transoxania to benefit the learned community.[28]

Muhammad bin Husayn's academic centre was such an excellent one that it carried Prophet Muhammad's letters written to different authoritative men and tribal chiefs in their original form. Likewise the statements of Hazrat 'Ali, Imam Hassan and Imam Husayn also added to the richness of this centre. The valuable material on Islamic jurisprudence, *'ilm al-*

---

[27] Tahir, op. cit., p. 418.

[28] S. Saulat, *Milit-i-Islamiyah ki Mukhtasar Tarikh*, Delhi, 1994, vol. III, p. 172.

kalam and Prophetic traditions was written on Khurasani, Chinese and Egyptian paper, which was copied and carried to distant provinces of Mamun's caliphate.[29] Among the celebrated intellectual centres, Samarkand occupies an inimitable place for the cultivation and continuation of the Islamic intellectual tradition. To this matchless city of Central Asia is attributed an excellent academic atmosphere that retained Islamic literary culture for centuries together. It is this city where the Muslims established the first-paper making industry during the Umayyad period (CE 661–750). From here was supplied the paper to other parts of the caliphate to transmit the academic tradition to different corners of the world. This process strengthened the establishment of *kutub khana*s where the skilled copiers and calligraphers (*khattat*) improved the standard of writing, printing and binding. The city of Samarkand remained a great centre of learning in almost all the branches of Islamic religious and social sciences especially during the Abbasid, the Samanid, Khawarizmshahi and Mongol periods. In the reign of Ulug Beg (AH 767–827), an extraordinary, *Rasd-gah* (observatory) was established in this city, where the eminent scholars like 'Alauddin 'Ali Qushaji, the commentator of the *Tajrid* (book of fundamentals regarding jurisprudence), Qazi Zadah Rumi, Gayathudin Jamshed and Mo'inuddin of Kashan worked in collaboration and produced astronomical tables, day–night duration charts, seasonal calendars and equipment to determine the cardinal directions as well as the sea routes.[30]

In CE 1257, Nasiruddin Tusi (CE 1200-74), established a *kutub khana* and an observatory adjacent to it at Maragah. It was a vigorous centre where the scholars of almost all the fields contributed respectively. The library of this academic centre

[29] *Ma'arif*, Delhi, 1984, vol. 134, pp. 352-53.

[30] Ibid., p. 354.

was extremely rich and comprised of 400,000 books compiled by the scholars of jurisprudence, grammar, astronomy, logic, arts, and physical and natural sciences.[31]

The city of Samarkand remained an excellent centre of Islamic jurisprudence as well; it is this city where the jurists like Qays bin Ishaq Samarqandi (d. AH 527) lived and taught the science of Islamic jurisprudence. He was a grand jurist, who acquired the knowledge from Imam Jurjani, recognized by his contemporaries as *Hujjat al-Islam* (the authority of Islam). Ahmad bin 'Umar Samarqandi (d. AH 552) is another great jurist who nourished the scholarly tradition and transmitted a good number of juristic compilations to the coming generations. 'Ali bin Muhammad Asbijabi (d. AH 535), a famous commentator of *al-Ziyadat*, *al-Mabsut* and *al-Jami al-Sagir*, is also reported to have served in this city for years together.[32]

The intellectual centres of Samarkand especially at Rigistan, Shir Darr and Tilla Rari containing *madrasa*s and *kutub khana*s have been mentioned with the celebral depiction in the Muslim chronicles. They had attained a benchmark in the then world academics and possessed matchless tradition as well as facilities for the venture of seeking knowledge.[33]

The famous city of Bukhara was a matchless pearl among the cities of Muslim caliphate. It has served as a prestigious centre of academic excellence during the Abbasid, Samanid and Khawarizmshahi periods. The Samanid rule (CE 874–1005) has been a hallmark in the history of Mawara al-Nahr. It opened an unsullied chapter for academic excellence and architecture in Central Asia. In addition to the intellectual persuits, the entire region's history is known for the great

---

[31] Taj-ud-Din Subki, *Tabaqat al-Shafiyah al-Kubra*, Cairo, vol. III, p. 117.

[32] Narakhshi, *Tarikh-i-Bukhara*, tr. Frye, Cambridge, 1954, p. 101.

[33] *Ma'arif*, op. cit., vol. 134, p. 355.

architectural plan. During the period of Samanids; Bukhara took pride and has been mentioned as Qubbat al-Islam (the identity of Islam).[34] Ibn Battuta (CE 1304-77), a reputed traveller and historian has given a scholarly account during his visit to Bukhara.[35] He, during his stay in Bukhara, visited many mausoleums and tombs of the famous traditionists and jurists of this city.[36] He was wonder-struck on seeing the names and titles of the works compiled by these scholars inscribed on stone-plates adjacent to these tombs.[37] During the Samanid regime, Bukhara took also pride of being the capital of Samanid domain for about two centuries.[38] A great number of jurists, traditionists, poets, writers, artisans and craftsmen flocked and flourished here during the Samanid regime.[39]

The reputed *fuqaha* (jurists), who flourished in Bukhara during second, third and fourth century AH, were Muhammad bin Salam Bayqandi, 'Abdullah bin Muhammad Musandi, Muhammad bin 'Urwah, Harun bin Shagaf, Sahal bin Sharuzia Bukhari, 'Ubeydullah bin Wasil, Qasim bin Zakariya Matruz, Abu Qureysh, Hashid bin Isma'il Bukhari, Ishaq bin Dawud, Muhammad bin 'Abdullah bin Junayd, Muhammad bin Musa, Jaf'ar bin Muhammad Neshapuri, Abu Bakr bin Daw'ud, Abu al-Qasim Bhagwi, Abu Muhammad bin Sa'id, Muhammad bin Harun Hazrami and Husayn bin 'Aamili.[40] The jurists mentioned have been recognized by their contemporaries as great figures having strong grip over varied disciplines of the

---

34 *Dairat al-Ma'arif*, Danishgah-i-Punjab, Lahore, 1984, vol. I, p. 104.

35 Ibid., p. 905.

36 William B. Fisher et al., *The Cambridge History of Iran*, Cambridge, 1968-89, vol. IV, p. 476.

37 Haji Khalifah, op. cit., vol. II, p. 381.

38 *Dairat al-Ma'arif*, vol. I, p. 904.

39 Ibid., p. 905.

40 P.K. Hitti, *History of the Arabs*, London, 1970, p. 709.

Islamic sciences. The students, from different regions of the Muslim world used to flock round them in *majalis* (gatherings), *halqas* (sittings) and *masajids* (mosques) in order to seek the brilliant knowledge of *hadith* and *fiqh* in addition to the general course curriculam.[41]

The towering jurists and scholars who flourished in Bukhara and contributed to the venture of Islamic jurisprudence include the disciples of Imam Muhammad bin Salam Bayqandi, 'Abdullah bin Muhammad Musandi, Muhammad bin 'Urwah, Harun bin Shagaf and Sahal bin Sharuzia Bukhari.[42] The *marwiyat* (narrations) and *isnad* (transmitting authority) of 'Ubeydullah bin Wasil, Qasim bin Zakariya Matruz, Abu Qureysh, Hashid bin Isma'il Bukhari, Ishaq bin Dawud, Muhammad bin 'Abdullah bin Junayd, Muhammad bin Musa, Jaf'ar bin Muhammad Neshapuri, Abu Bakr bin Daw'ud, Abu al-Qasim Bhagwi, Abu Muhammad bin Sa'id, Muhammad bin Harun Hazrami and Husayn bin 'Aamili also added splendour to the science of Islamic jurisprudence in the entire region of Mawara al-Nahr.[43]

Burhan al-A'imah 'Umar bin 'Abd al-'Aziz bin Mazah (d. AH 532) has been a grand jurist as well as a versatile scholar of Bukhara. He compiled treatises on a variety of disciplines that included *'ilm al-kalam* (philosophy) and *fiqh* (jurisprudence). Among his compilations on jurisprudence are *Fatawa al-Kubra, Fatawa al-Sugra* and *Sharah Jami al-Sagir*.[44]

Ahmad bin 'Abd al-'Aziz (AH 423) a famous commentrator on principles of jurisprudence (*usul al-fiqh*) wrote a number of books and delivered lectures on *fiqh* in the mosque of Bukhara

---

[41] *Dairat al-Ma'arif*, op. cit., vol. I, p. 908.

[42] Ibid., p. 358.

[43] Ibid., p. 359.

[44] S. Sulayman Nadvi, *Islam Aur Mustashriqin*, Ma'arif, Delhi, 1985, vol. 135, p. 26.

and a considerable number of scholars and students flocked around him to transmit the knowledge of Sha'riah to the forthcoming generations.[45]

Sheikh Muhammad bin 'Abd al-Rehman Bukhari (d. AH 546), commonly known as "Zahid al-'Aml", was a reputed scholar who made addition to the scholarly tradition in Central Asia. He wrote on the subjects which included the science of jurisprudence and made considerable addition to *usul al-fiqh* methodology. He wrote a voluminous commentary on Quran and tried to present Quranic impressions in support to the juristic instruments of *istidlal, istehsan* and *ijma.* He identified *taghaur* (change) as an ultimate principle that determines the fate of a legal verdict. To him the Quranic injections can never contradict with any natural phenomenon and social evolution.[46]

The renowned scholars, Sheikh 'Uthman bin 'Ali Bakandi and Muhammad bin Mahmud Tarazi (d. AH 570) also belonged to the same region and had established distinguished academic centres and seminaries in Bukhara.[47] Both the scholars have been mentioned as the forerunners of the Islamic legal tradition and contributed to this field by virtue of writing commentaries to a number of juristic treatises.[48]

Moreover, the 'Mir-i-Arab' Madrasa at Bukhara (est. CE 942), Ulug Bey Madrasa and Lab-i-Hawd were the prestigious centres of academic excellence during tenth and eleventh centuries CE which are noted for the dissemination of Islamic knowledge.[49] Their fame and academic endeavour have been endorsed even by the European academicians and literary circles. The Ilkhanids, Timurids and Mongols also constructed

[45] *Encyclopaedia of Islam*, vol. IV, p. 558.

[46] Ibid., p. 559

[47] Gangohi, *Zafr al-Muhasilin*, Deoband, 1996, p. 280.

[48] Haji Khalifah, op. cit., vol. IV, p. 1632.

[49] Gangohi, op. cit., p. 282.

and established seminaries during thirteenth, fourteenth and fifteenth centuries.[50] The Mongol emperor Halugu's mother built two *madrasas* in Bukhara, where 1,000 students studied different branches of Islamic sciences from reputed intellectuals.[51]

Before the Russian Revolution of 1917, there were 380 *madrasas* in Bukhara where 40,000 students were on rolls.[52] In Turkistan, Siberia, Adal, Aural and Qafqaz the number of religious institutions extended to 1,075.[53] These institutions were managed and administered by the Auqaf and the teachers in these institutions were paid handsome salaries.[54]

The *wilayat* (province) of Farghana has also been a famous and reputed centre of Islamic intellectualism in Central Asia. The Muslim historians trace its academic and scholastic activities since CE 850.[55] Its rich academic tradition flourished to the adjacent provinces. 'Umar bin Haseeb Zindramasi (sixth century AH) was the chief *qazi* of Farghana. He was a great jurist and reputed scholar of *tafsir* (exegesis) and *hadith*. He annotated Qazi Ahmad bin 'Abd al-Aziz's book '*Masa'il al-Asrar* and added incredible notes to it.[56]

Minhaj al-Shari'ah Muhammad bin Muhammad was a towering scholar and jurist. He used to deliver lectures on *hadith* and *fiqh* in Farghana mosque.[57] 'Abul Ma'ani Zahir-ud-din and Sheikh 'Usman bin Ibrahim were also the natives of Farghana who associated themselves with the academic centres here and

[50] Gangohi, op. cit., p. 282.

[51] Ahmad bin Muhammad, *Usul al-Shashi*, Beirut, 1982, pp. 6-7.

[52] Gangohi, op. cit., p. 283.

[53] Bukhari, *Maqalat al-Nabigah*, Delhi, 1999, p. 9.

[54] Gangohi, op. cit., p. 267.

[55] Al-Qarshi, *Jawahar al-Muziah*, Cairo, 1896, vol. I, p. 188.

[56] Haji Khalifah, op. cit., vol. III, p. 283.

[57] Ibn Najim, *Bahr al-Raiq*, Delhi, 1932, vol. II, p. 222.

taught the science of Islamic jurisprudence. They exclusively contributed to the Islamic literary tradition in this region and served the cause of Islamic knowledge.[58]

The city of Merghinan was very much prolific regarding the dissemination of Islamic knowledge. Being a great centre of learning, reputed figures and intellectuals could be seen in every walk of life. The scholars emerging from this soil attained fame and attracted disciples from the far-off places of the caliphate.[59] The reputed scholars of *hadith* and *fiqh* flourished here and made valuable contribution to their respective fields.[60] Burhanudin 'Ali bin Abu Bakr Merghinani (d. AH 539), the author of celebrated *Al-Hidayah*, 'Abdullah bin Abi al-Fath Khanqahi, Fazlullah Asfurqani, Zahir-ud-din Hassan bin 'Ali, famous disciple of Imam Tirmizi, Zia ud-din Sa'ad bin Asad are among the reputed scholars of *hadith* and jurisprudence who established themselves in Marghinan.[61] Abu-Hafs 'Umar bin 'Ali, the author of *Jawahar al-Fiqh* and *al-Fawa'id*,[62] and Sheikh Imadudin, the author of *'Adab al-Qazi'*, were also the natives of Merghinan.[63]

The cities Shash, Osh and Rushdan were also famous for Islamic institutions and the men of letters in diverse fields flourished in these cities.[64] The reputed scholar of *ilm al-usul al-fiqh*, Ahmad bin Muhammad Shashi (d. AH 325), the author of celebrated work *Usul al-Shashi*, Naseer bin Muhammad Sulaiman Oshi (AH 402), Muhammad bin Ahmad (AH 356) and Abu Bakr bin Hatam Rushdani (AH 367) were from these regions whose

---

58 Haji Khalifah, op. cit., vol. III, p. 107.

59 *Encyclopaedia of Islam*, vol. IV, p. 507.

60 Haji Khalifah, op. cit., vol. II, p. 1008.

61 Ibid., vol. III, p. 1009.

62 Gangohi, op. cit., p. 269.

63 Ibid.

64 Ibid., p. 262.

contribution to Islamic jurisprudence, *hadith* and legal theory could never be underestimated.[65]

The institutional influences of Merv and Khiva could also be seen in the academic circles of Mawara al-Nahr. Both the cities have remained hubs for the study of *hadith* and Islamic jurisprudence.[66] Muhammad bin Abu Bakr was a great scholar of Merv who contributed a lot in the field of jurisprudence.[67] 'Ali bin Ahmad, the author of *Al-Tafsir al-Wasit* belonged to this city.[68] Sheikh Zia ud-din Muhammad bin Husayn (d. 570), a famous narrator of *Sahih al-Muslim, Kitab al-Risalah* and *Kitab al-Tamhid* remained in Khiva and benefited the learned community by virtue of compiling treatises on Islamic jurisprudence.[69]

Muhammad bin Hassan bin Mas'ud (d. AH 562), flourished in Merv, visited Khiva and compiled *Sharah Maa'ni al-Aasar*.[70] Abul Fath Muhammad bin 'Abdul Rehman Maruzi (d. AH 565), a famous disciple of Imam al-Bukhari established himself in Merv and delivered lectures on *Al-Jami Sahih al-Bukhari*.[71] Merv and Khiva, as reported by the scholarly evidences, went on side to side to carry the tradition of Islamic knowledge tradition to diverse directions of the Muslim domain.[72]

Balkh and Herat were also the prestigious seats of learning in Mawara al-Nahr.[73] The Madrasa Nizamia in Balkh and Herat were extremely prolific as well as professional caring for the

---

65 Gangohi, op. cit., p. 270.

66 Ibid., p. 271.

67 Ibid.

68 Ibid., p. 279.

69 Al-Qarshi, op. cit., vol. II, p. 193.

70 Haji Khalifah, op. cit., vol. III, p. 118.

71 Ibid., p. 219.

72 Al-Qarshi, op. cit., vol. I, p. 67.

73 Gangohi, op. cit., p. 277.

regulation of the scholarly persuits.[74] Qazi Sa'eed bin Yusuf al-Hanafi (AH 502) held the chair of *muhadith*, Zia al-Islam 'Umar bin Muhammad (AH 409) held the seat of *faqih*, Muhammad bin Muhammad (AH 514) held the seat of *qazi* and *faqih* during sixth century AH.[75] These scholars contributed to the diverse fields of Islamic learning and retained the venture of Islamic professionalism for centuries together.[76] Maki bin Ibrahim (d. AH 302), Yehya bin Kathir (AH 298), Qutaybah (AH 218), Muhammad bin Shuj'a Balkhi (d. AH 266), Imam Abu Ja'far Balkhi (d. 362) and Mo'in al-Haravi (AH 344) also served in Balkh and Herat to impart the knowledge of Islam to the upcoming generations.[77]

Tirmiz, a great city of Mawara al-Nahr has also been a reputed centre for Islamic knowledge tradition. The city has been praised by the title "Madint al-Rijal" (city of the learned).[78] The famous traditionist and compiler of celebrated work in *hadith*, *Jam'i al-Tirmizi* Abu 'Isa Muhammad al-Tirmizi (d. AH 279) was a native of this city. He acquired his knowledge from different scholars who flourished here during third century AH.[79] The distinguished traditionists and jurists from this city also include 'Abdul 'Abas Muhammad bin Ahmad, Al-Maruzi, Ahmad bin Yusuf Nasafi, Dawud bin Nasr Bazudi, Hatham bin Kalib al-Shahi, Abu Hamid Ahmad Maduzi, 'Abd bin Muhammad and Muhammad bin Mehmood.[80]

Madrasas and other academic institutions of Neshapur have been discussed widely due of their well-equipped management

---

74 Gangohi, op. cit., p. 278.

75 Ibid.

76 Haji Khalifah, op. cit., vol. III, p. 221.

77 Ibid.

78 Ibid., p. 223.

79 Umar Raza Kahalah, *Mujam al-Mualifin*, Damascus, 1957, vol. II, p. 164.

80 Gangohi, op. cit., p. 287.

and academic excellence.[81] The first *madrasa* established in this city was "Madrasah al-Bayhaqiyah" (f. AH 458/CE 1066),[82] by Imam Bayhaqi a great scholar of *hadith*.[83] The reputed biographer and historian, Ibn Khalikan reports us that the prestigious institutions of Neshapur included Madrasa al-Saadiyah founded by Amir Naser in CE 999,[84] Madrasah al-Nizamiyah (f. AH 456),[85] Madrasah al-Bayhaqiyah (f. AH 458)[86] and Madrasah al-Nasriyah which were great centres of learning during fifth century AH. In these highly-administered institutions, ample scholastic facilities, libraries and men of knowledge remained available for the scholarly community. These institutions were highly prolific and equipped with valuable material in almost all the fields of knowledge.[87] The academic approaches of the scholars here added to the magnificent contribution for the socio-political urgencies. These approaches influenced and opened various social and political institutions during the Abbasid period.[88]

The academic institutions of Neshapur have been discussed widely mainly due to their diverse curriculum and inter-disciplinary scholastic approach. The well-equipped management, facilities and academic excellence attracted a huge number of students to study here.[89] In the Nizamiyah Madrasa of Neshapur a grand mosque and a library adjacent

---

81 Gangohi, op. cit., p. 288.

82 Umar Raza Kahalah, op. cit., p. 167.

83 Haji Khalifah, op. cit., vol. III, p. 121.

84 Gangohi, op. cit., p. 288.

85 Ibid.

86 Ibid., p. 289.

87 Ibn Qatlubigah, *Taj al-Tarajim fi Tabaqat al-Hanafiyah*, Baghdad, 1962, p. 162.

88 Gangohi, op. cit., p. 295.

89 Zarkali, *Al-A'lam*, Beirut, 1953, vol. II, p. 138.

to it provided valuable material to the scholars for undertaking advance study into various disciplines.[90] It is from this soil that the distinguished scholars and jurists like Sheikh Abu Hafs Hadad, Abu 'Ali Daqaq, Abu Muhammad bin 'Ata Yehya Jawahari, Ibn Rahawya, Thaclbi, 'Umar Khayam, Hussayn Ma'mai, al-Naziri, al-Aahali and al-Aagahi emerged.[91]

When Taj al-Mulk (d. CE 1073), founded prestigious Madrasa Shatibiyah in Baghdad, Madrasa Ma'ani and Madrasa Shatibiyah had already been established in Neshapur some years earlier.[92] These institutions had teachers for Quran, *hadith, fiqh* and *falkiyat* (astronomy).[93] Attached to them were the *kutub khanas, hamams, mustashfas* and *matbakhs*.[94] There was a clock at the entrance, a physician to take care of students and an administrator for the overall supervision of the academic activities.[95]

The academic institutions established in Transoxania, Persia and eastern lands of the Muslim caliphate depicted the highly scholastic atmosphere. They had maintained prolific connections with those of Arabia and Iraq in terms of the nature of activities, curriculum and courses of the study.[96] These reputed institutions produced socio-legal experts such as *muftis* (jurisconsults), *faqihs* (jurists), *umal* (tax collectors) and *qazis* (judges) who got involved in the public administration for civil services.[97] With expansion of the prolification and Muslim academia, some significant institutions came into

---

90 Gangohi, op. cit., p. 294.

91 Haji Khalifah, op. cit., vol. IV, p. 372.

92 Ibid.

93 Ibid., p. 373.

94 Ibid.

95 Ibid., p. 374.

96 *Encyclopaedia of Islam*, vol. IV, p. 558.

97 *Dairat al-Ma'arif*, vol. I, p. 904.

existence especially *dar al-hadith*.[98] In this institution, *muhadith* was raised to the level of *muddaris* in *madrasas*.[99] The institution of *dar al-hadith* served to bring together students of all *madhab*s and devised the courses of law and ancillary sciences for the students.[100] The students of each *madhab* were taught separately and scholars of different *madhab* would teach the students of their respective fields for a fixed period.[101]

Among the other Islamic conventional establishments of this era were the institution of *dar al-quran*, *khanaqah* and *zawiyah*, where the aspirants could attain the knowledge and spiritual guidance. The trainees in these scholarly circles would come out having command over the scholastic as well as spiritual excellence.[102] In "Khanaqah-i-Shaykhun", founded in AH 756/ CE 1355, an extensive course of lectures, *fiqh* according to all four *madahibs*, *hadith* and the tradition of *iqra* (formal learning), was given.[103] The scholars of various subjects and disciplines were having an intense care for the institution's well-being as well as for scholarly activities performed there.[104] In the formal discourse, the general designation for a master was "Sheikh", when used with a compliment, the term designated the master of various fields, for example "Sheikh al-Qirat" for the professor of Quranic studies, "Sheikh al-Hadith" was the designation of a professor teaching prophetic traditions and was considered an authority in his respective field.[105] The term

98 *Encyclopaedia of Islam*, vol. IV, p. 559.

99 Ibid.

100 Ibid.

101 'Ali bin Abu Bakr Marghinani, *Al-Hidayah*, Delhi, 1994, vol. I, Table of Contents, p. 3.

102 N.J. Coulson, *A History of Islamic Law*, Edinburgh, 1990, p. 103.

103 Ibid., p. 67.

104 *Dairat al-Ma'arif*, op. cit., vol. IV, p. 560.

105 Ibid.

rais was applied to any scholar who had reached the summit of his field in his locality.[106] This term was used especially in the field of teaching the Islamic law.[107]

In the academic institutions of Neshapur, *rais* was assisted by a deputy called *naib rais* who taught during the absence of *rais*.[108] Consequently, in the *madrasa*s of Mawara al-Nahr, the term used to designate the director of an institution was Sheikh al-Ribat who would initiate all the scholarly persuits and would also be responsible for the administrative affairs of the institution.[109]

The expert of Islamic jurisprudence (*faqih*) or the professor of law was having a special status and extreme honour in the scholarly community.[110] To obtain *ijazah* (licence) to teach law, one had to study many years under a jurist or professor of law, become proficient in the scholastic method of disputation and build up with a vast knowledge of resolving the disputes with mind and skill.[111] Then one had to successfully defend his thesis or opinion by sound reasoning.[112] More rarely a law student could study under as many as five professors, but the process was always the same that was to defend his thesis by absolute skill and sound reasoning in light of the primary sources.[113] After mastering this skill, a student was given the status of *rais* or *mu'id* (assistant to cross-check) or *mufid* (scholar to add necessary notes over a legal verdict), and provided an *ijazah* attesting his competence in the field of Islamic law.[114]

---

106 Dairah al-Ma'arif, op. cit., vol. IV, p. 561.

107 *Encyclopaedia of Islam*, vol. IV, p. 569.

108 Ibid., p. 561.

109 Ibid., p. 562.

110 Ibid.

111 Ibid., p. 563.

112 'Ali bin Abu Bakr Marghinani, *Al-Hidayah*, Delhi, 1994, vol. I, p. 3.

113 Ibid.

114 Ibid.

The alumni emerging from these reputed institutions were extremely versatile and had a strong grip over the explanation as well as deep insight into the social occurrences. Their legal insight was so effective and profound that they could determine the fate of any upcoming issue with absolute legal skill and interpretation. The spectacular works compiled by the reputed scholars of Islamic jurisprudence emerged with acute social spirit to overcome any social occurrence without any difficulty. Appearently, with this notion the science of Islamic jurisprudence explored its vast canvas for the study of socio-economic and legal phenomena.[115]

The profound compilations and treatises authored in this direction contained valuable material for the precepts concerning the socio-institutions including *nikah* (marriage), *talaq* (divorce), *utaq* (manumission of slaves), *aiman* (laws of vows), *hudud* (laws of crimes and punishments), *taz'ir* (laws of unspecified punishments), *sirkah* (laws of theft), *laqit* (laws of qundlings), *luqtah* (laws of trove), *aabaq* (laws related to absconding of slaves and prisoners of war), *mafqud* (laws related to missing persons), *shirkah* (laws of partnership or company law), *waqf* (laws of trurts), *bayu* (laws of contracts and transactions or sales), *kafalah* (laws of bails), *hawalah* (laws of transfer of debts), *aadab al-qazi* (procedural laws of duties of judges), *'aariyah* (laws of loans), *wadi'ah* (laws of deposits), *muzaribah* (laws of co-partnership in profits of stock and labour), *sulah* (laws of compositions), *wakalah* (laws of agency), *dawa* (laws of claims), *shihadah* (laws of evidence), *raju an al-shihadah* (laws of retraction of evidence), *ushribah* (laws of prohibition of liquors), *ahya al-mawat* (laws of cultivation of waste lands), *qismah* (laws of partition), *shufa'ah* (laws of pre-emption), *zira'ah* (laws of cultivation), *ghazab* (laws of usurpation), *rahn* (laws of powns), *wasayah* (laws of treatment

[115] 'Ali bin Abu Bakr Marghinani, *Al-Hidayah*, Delhi, 1994, vol. I, p. 4.

of wills), *ma'aqil* (laws of levying of fines), *janayat* (offences against the persons or criminal law) and *diyat* (law of torts; law of fines and damages).[116]

All the schools of Islamic law tried to manifest their scholarship and interpretations as they thought fit to the emerging social needs. With the expansion of the caliphate beyond Arabia, the Muslim academia evolved extensively to gear up with the social set-up as well as with the exploration of the innovative methodologies in diverse fields of knowledge. This intellectual process resulted in reallocation of the legal theory as per the exegent circumstances harmonizing revelation with the applied human reason. All this happened by virtue of concentration upon the *fiqh* material, sources and mode of imparting legal expertise while codifying the Shari'ah laws.[117] Again, it was extremely by the concern, concentration and understanding of the Muslim jurists that the public administration got sufficient ideological, constitutional and legal stuff rooted in the Islamic fundamentals.[118]

116 'Ali bin Abu Bakr Marghinani, *Al-Hidayah*, Delhi, 1994, vol. I, p. 4.

117 *Encyclopaedia of Islam*, vol. IV, p. 570.

118 Tahir, op. cit., p. 419.

6

Conclusion

THE science of Islamic jurisprudence (*'ilm al-fiqh*) is a vast and dynamic field that emerged within the realm of primary sources of law, namely, Quran and Sunnah. This discipline is undoubtly a significant component of the Islamic knowledge system that evolved to interpret the accurate understanding of Quran and Sunnah or what is technically termed as *tafaquh fi al-din* (absolute understanding of the commandments of Shari'ah). Islamic jurisprudence as a special branch of the Islamic sciences has evolved to resolve various social issues besides making the religious commandments and their objectives (*maqasid*) clear to the society. As already discussed, this discipline developed from a variety of sources identified within the Islamic legal theory. The social application of the discipline is inevitable as it made the law relevant to the changing circumstances. The expertise involved to deduct from the sources of law has made Muslim jurists aware of the fact that the law must be in conformation with the existing social scenario. It is through this aspect and spirit that the law can guide the Muslim society and maintain its character in existing and future circumstances. With this undissoluble legal character, Islamic jurisprudence has contributed a lot to the understanding of social phenomenon and its resolution through the revealed precepts. The Islamic knowledge system has shaped the face of society and strengthened the Muslim caliphate (*khilafah*) by developing institutions responsible for its growth and sustenance.

Islamic sciences (*'ulum*) have a peculiar nature both in presenting the world-view as well as in socio-legal perspective. The entire realm of the Islamic knowledge system shares its roots with the changing face of the society besides being fundamentally rooted in the revealed tradition. Islam's triumph over Arabia and beyond is, in fact, an ample proof that as a religion and social philosophy, Islam made its adherents compatible with other civilizations and cultures existing at that time. Islam's entrance to Central Asia can be treated as one of the solid examples in this direction. The history of the development of Islamic sciences is evident to the fact that the geographical region, Mawara al-Nahr (Transoxania) or what now is Central Asia has a gigantic share for the cultivation as well as for the restoration of the Islamic sciences (*'ulum al-islami*) since second century AH/eighth century CE.

As a comprehensive, categoric and relevant system, the development of Islamic jurisprudence (*fiqh*) can be traced from various regions of the Muslim caliphate (*khilafah*) and divided into various distinct phases enabling it to assume a permanent structure in the Islamic knowledge system. In its initial stage, the Quranic revelations got applied in the very presence of Prophet Muhammad (SAW) and society had nothing to worry about regarding the execution of the socio-legal issues. The prophet himself would explain all the necessary content of a revealed commandment (*hukm*) as well as its mode of application. This sort of direct legislation extended from AH 1/CE 622 to AH 10/CE 632 and during this significant period legislation took place through Quranic revelations and instructions elaborated by Prophet Muhammad (SAW) himself.

The second phase extends from Prophet's passing away (AH 10/CE 632) and would cover time of the companions (*suhabah*) and their successors (*taba'in*). This crucial period is earmarked with the collection of decisions, instructions and resolutions carried out by Prophet Muhammad (SAW), legislation under the guidance of first four caliphs (*Khulafa-al-Rashidun*) and the collections by some reputed companions during this period. All this exersion resulted in the formulation of the Islamic legal theory in an absolute legislative form. The third phase of the legal theory (second century AH/eighth century CE) witnessed incredible social occurrences and trends regarding interpretation as well as the application of the legal theory by the Muslim jurists (*fuqaha*). The knowledge of juristic injunctions (*ahkam al-shara'i*) got momentum and various schools of the legal thought emerged with certain methodologies. The methodological differences of various schools of thought can be witnessed in the works pertaining to *usul al-fiqh* where the noted jurists exerted to interpret the legal theory as per the circumstantial understanding.

It is worth to mention here that the process of the expansion of Islam beyond Arabia brought novel experiences to Muslims. This expansion put forth new dimensions to the legal theory broadening its scope for interpreting the social phenomenon in a much wider perspective. At this juncture the Muslim *fuqaha* had to confront and respond to a variety of social issues mostly not witnessed during the lifetime of the Prophet (SAW) or the period of the *Khulafa-al-Rashidun* (rightly guided caliphs). The jurists at that time approached the basic sources of law through a variety of legal tools identified within the spirit of Quran and Sunnah.

In fact, the literature compiled on *usul al-fiqh* or *fiqh* especially during third and fourth century AH reveals that the legal theory in Islam is not a rigid system of legal codes or a stagnant judicial procedure, rather a comprehensive legal system based upon the concept of revelation (*wahy*), reason (*'aql*) and welfare (*falah*). Hence the objective of Islamic jurisprudence is to address, interpret and resolve all such issues where the revealed text seems allegoric or needs further explanation (*tashrih*) or the idea as how a particular injunction is to be applied in its socio-legal perspective. Absolutely, it is due to this particular intent that the science of Islamic jurisprudence attained all the necessary features required to construct a socio-legal mechanism upon the Islamic ideals. The egalitarian and universal outlook of the Islamic legal theory surpassed all the existing legal codes due to its social workability and prudence. The socio-political ambience of the non-Arab lands especially Central Asia stimulated various organs of the social institutions and enabled the Islamic legal science to grow fully to attain the universal character.

The Central Asian territory referred in the Islamic chronicals as Mawara al-Nahr, since its integration to the Islamic caliphate in CE 715 by Umayyads (CE 661–750), remained as a hub of Islamic intellectualism and the scholars of this region contributed an immense share to the Islamic civilization. The history of the Muslim intellectual legacy here is evident to the fact that the scholars of this region solely participated in the scholarly infatuation and inspired the men of letters to cultivate literary tradition in far-off regions of the Muslim caliphate. The interaction with a variety of cultures and human experiences widened the scope of Islamic legal theory and exposed it to a series of societal expressions alien to the predecessors (*salf*). The concept of change and social service remained the primary concern of the Islamic jurisprudence enabling it to perform as a channel of proper guidance to the society. Since its formulation, the Islamic legal theory accommodated and conformed a number of social occurrences that emerged as a result of social change or expansion. Again, it is the universal character of the Islamic legal theory that it accommodated a variety of characters not experienced by *salf* or in the earlier compilations. Hence the resolution of the socio-legal issues in the absence of a clear commandment was the profound concern of Islamic jurisprudence.

In fact, the knowledge and the societies all over the world are growing very fast. At present, the Muslim world is facing intellectual, political, and socio-economic crises. In the prevailing circumstances, the Muslims cannot run away from the modern intellectual and scientific advances and take refuge in traditional mode of acquiring knowledge, rather they have to move forward without getting cut-off from their glorious past. The Muslim scholars and jurists have to play a vital role for reallocation of the studies in Islam. Hence, the discipline of Islamic jurisprudence is still evolving to accommodate and deliberate upon a number of issues never experienced before. Modern concepts, theories and ideas do make their impact on our ways of thinking and often shape up our perceptions accordingly. At this very juncture it is inevitable to interpret and relate the Islamic tenets as per the circumstantial needs. The composition of the Islamic knowledge system, although divinely ordained, has to overcome the emerging social needs and excessive social contacts in the contemporary world.

The outcome of the socio-cultural interaction and general benefit of the social contacts has remained a crucial topic in Islamic jurisprudence. Thus, in the Islamic legal theory, the socio-ethical content has been thoroughly debated and mentioned under the legal themes like *istehsan* (juristic equality), *istislah* (public good) or *masaliah al-mursalah* (public interest). The nature and prelude of these terms are connected with the social experiences beneficial to the human society without contradicting the Islamic value system. These concepts represent and carry the innovative tendency to reorient Islamic jurisprudence as per the exigent socio-legal prespective. This evolutionary and distinctive character makes Islamic legal theory current as well as dynamic. The Islamic legal theory matches the standard of social workability and has the capacity to deduce for the emerging social needs by exercising the institution of consensus (*ijma*) and exersion (*ijtihad*).

The *Fuqaha* utilized their utmost intellectual worth to ensure the maximum socio-legal benefit while deducing law from a variety of generally accepted sources. The deduction of the legal precepts and methodology has been a monumental endeavour of the Muslim jurists. The jurists, thus having command over the text, its possible interpretations and social workability made valuable contribution to legal theory and its application. Obviously, it is the ultimate relationship between the socio-religious and judicial backgrounds that the scope of Islamic jurisprudence has extremely amplified and maintained connection between the society and the divine command.

The Muslim jurists and scholars of the Central Asia authored and annotated legal treatises with the same spirit. They exposed their utmost concern to deal with the problems that arise from social interaction enlarging the scope for debate or rethinking the possibilities within a legal verdict. The socio-political developments, especially during the Umayyad (CE 661–750), Abbasid (CE 750–1258) and the Samanid (CE 874–1005) periods were having perpetual significance. The socio-economic practices during these eras have indeed influenced and shaped the discourse of legal theory in Islam. It was during this period that the interaction with different cultures, ethnic groups and regions widened the scope of Islamic legal discourse enabling it to assume a standardized universal character. The Muslim legal experts took inspirations from the changing facet of societies and interpreted legal discourse to suit the circumstances. The Muslim jurists were certain in believeing that Islamic jurisprudence must reveal the fate of confronting situations (*mahazr*) with an absolute potential. The ultimate aim of law is to identify or unveil a commandment (*hukm al-shara'i*) in relation to its social adaptability. This is how the Muslim jurists approached and deduced from the concept of social change. The flow of information with regard to the development of Islamic jurisprudence was not only adopted by the Muslim jurists but also contributed to this flow of information by virtue of writing commentaries, selective principles and methods to study the subject with its contemporary relevance. The mode of operating upon the sources, consideration of overall socio-political and legal scenarios, its evaluation by means of consensus (*ijma*) and analogy (*qiyas*), absolutely were the foremost contribution of the Muslim jurists. As a result, a scholarly conviction full of socio-legal expertise gave birth to an evolving tradition surpassing world's utmost judicial codes and mechanisms. Again, it was ultimately this passion that the Muslim jurists compiled renowned works helping in the codification of law as well as in classification of the sanctions in the legal science.

The scholars discussed with reference to Central Asia have done a marvellous contribution to the field of Islamic jurisprudence. Their significance and extraordinary role regarding the formulation and deduction of laws, from and in accordance with sources have been really considerable. They made an absolute legal exercise into the primary sources, books on *usul al-fiqh*, *qiyas* and *ijma*, and sanctioned definitions to a variety of socio-legal contents not reflected in the earlier phase of the Islamic history. These scholars, particularly in the Abbasid period (CE 750–1258), worked hand-in-hand in the official capacity, identified themselves with the system and explored the sources of law for the community benefits. This recognition and keen insight resulted in imparting the knowledge tradition, establishing institutions *par excellence* and resolving issues of socio-political and religious importance. Their role as "social activists" also added glamour to the socio-legal expertise in Islam and provided sufficient ideological content for legal deductions. The magnificent aspect of their contribution is validiating the concept of change (*taghaur*) and its impact over socio-legal institutions and interpretations. The Muslim jurists believed that the nature of laws changes with the changes in time (*wa yeta badal al-ahkam bi-tabdil al-azminah*). It is indeed this legal precept that has brought relevance as well as coherence to the science of Islamic jurisprudence. The Muslim jurists implied that the content (*asl*) and context (*tanazur*) of a legal verdict are to be properly understood. This scheme of socio-legal relativity can offer better results. The deductions experienced through this scheme can be utilized and interpreted for the social benefits (*maqasid*). The Muslim jurists who thought and wrote in a particular social environment are a valuable but not an ultimate binding upon the people who came centuries after them (*imkan al-ijtihad*). However, their methods of legal deduction and modes of operating upon the sources have a vital role in preparing laws for the present-day society and its social needs.

The Muslim jurists believed that Islam always remained a vibrant source of the social morality. It approaches the social phenomenon catering almost all the individual and community needs within a just social mechanism. The entire structure of the Islamic legal theory has been in consonance with the idea of social workability. It treats humans as the active social forces created to ensure justice (*'adl*) and benevolence (*rahmah*). While application of the legal or juristic directive, knowing a commandment is not the ultimate goal rather to understand its nature is more important which justifies its position of being lawful or unlawful. To act on laws, it becomes necessary to understand the reasons (*'ilat*) lying behind them and to know that what purpose or general interests they serve.

Muslim intellectuals, throughout their career studied Islamic sciences with the same spirit. The reputed centres of Islamic academic excellence were having great concern regarding dissemination of knowledge. The academic institutions established in Central Asia during the Abbasid period grew extensively due to their relevance and multi-dimensional character. In the prestigious centres, throughout the caliphate, religious, social and natural sciences were studied with an equal consideration without separation of one from the other. The Abbasid Caliph Mamun fortified the educational standards and paid special attention to the academic activities during his reign. This academic endeavour was carried on especially by the Samanid rulers who ruled Central Asia from CE 874–1105. Almost all the academic institutions were having adjacent mosques and libraries to promote the knowledge of Islam. The institutions had proper administration to facilitate the basic requirements as well as scholarships to the meritorious students. A special feature to note here is that, the scholars of various disciplines would work together in collaboration and would never indulge in any sort of intolerent activity that would result in defacement of the academic atmosphere.

The Central Asian territories, for centuries together, have remained under the domination and influence of the Arabs, Iranians and the Turks. Muslims, during that period, were less interested in the identity recognized by tribes and nationalities; rather they thought religion as the pivotal force that unites cultures and ethnicities and recognize them as *ummah*. The men of authority at that time were the pioneers of faith who would try to maintain the law of Islam (Shari'ah) in consultation with *'ulama* (scholars). Central Asia has been ruled by the dynasties that were not distinguished for their tribal affiliations, who did not inherit their thrones from their forefathers, nothing brought them to this position except their submission to Islam and their interest in promotion of the knowledge.

The academic and intellectual scenario of Central Asia got disturbed by two venomous invasions by Mongols in CE 1220 and 1258. The Russian invasions of Central Asian territories during eighteenth–twentieth centuries have also been noxious. The Russian occupation of Central Asian states has again challenged the efficacy of the Islamic institutions through a plan of socio-intellectual modernization resulting in the defacement of Islamic legacy and knowledge tradition. This plan has also endangered the socio-cultural commitment of the Muslims of this region with Islam. Indeed, this malpractice has proved to be much destructive as compared to the Mongol invasions of CE 1220 and 1258. The Mongols plundered cities, killed people and went back. The Russians, on the other hand, dominated this region to exploit their economy and to put a gradual end to Islamic legacy in this region. From CE 1901-90, the Muslim institutions suffered a lot as their existence had been considered an obstacle in the way of modernization as well as a hurdle for further extension of Soviet Union to Afghanistan and South Asia. This state of affairs remained until the disintegration of USSR in 1991.

With the emergence of independent Muslim states of Central Asia in 1991, Islamic institutions, be it social or intellectual got a chance to re-establish their ultimate Muslim character. Thus, the independent Muslim states of Central Asia have sustained the hope for preserving Islamic legacy as well as its move towards potential realization. In this regard the emergence of newly-born states is an unbelievable achievement. The reactivation and perseverance of Islamic legacy is very crucial as it has worked successfully here for centuries together. Islamic institutions and sciences have been successfully developed in this region and it would not be an exaggeration to characterize Islamic culture partly as Central Asian. But, the Islamic character of the institutions is to be planned and justified. Otherwise, it can be considered an obstacle in the wake of modernization. As a result, the system that contained the character of universal adaptability and acted as an effective tool for social mobilization for centuries together, will seem irrelevant and confusing. We must realize this issue and should approach the dynamism of Islam to cater and explore the current and emerging chellenges. Besides the sound agricultural base, the Central Asian Muslim economy is blessed with gold, minerals and substantial reserves of energy resources, but the question is, will this blessed territory would ever show the concern for Islamic spirit which had shaped its distinction throughout centuries. If this is achieved, the Central Asian Muslim states, really would be an ultimate example for reactivation of the Muslim creed and their possible advance towards peace, progress and prosperity in the modern times.

Bibliography

Primary Sources

Abbadi, Abu Asim, *Tabaqat al-Fuqaha*, Leiden: E.J. Brill, 1964.

Abu Hanifa, *Fiqh al-Akbar,* Hyderabad, AH 1349.

———, *Al-Musnad*, Saharanpur (UP), 1987.

Abu Yusuf, *Kitab al-Asar,* Lahore, AH 1366.

———, *Kitab al-Kharaj*, Egypt: Salfiya, AH 1352.

Abu Bakr, M., *Ahkam al-Quran*, Egypt, 1957.

Abu Hilal Askari, *Kitab al-Awail*, Egypt, AH 1317.

Abu Zuhra, *Abu Hanifa*, Delhi, 1987.

Al-Aini, *Al-Binayah*, Hyderabad, 1967.

Al-Asqalani, *Tehzib al-Tehzib*, Beirut, 1993.

Abu Dawud, *Al-Sunan*, Kanpur, 2 vols., 1928.

Al-Amadi, *Al-Ahkam*, Cairo, 4 vols., 1914.

Baghdadi, A. Qahir, *Usul al-Din*, Beirut, 1981.

Baghdadi, Al-Khateeb, *Al-Faqih*, Beirut, vol. II, 1975.

———, *Tarikh-i-Baghdad*, Lebanon, 1956.

Baghdadi, *Al-Qudoori*, Deoband, 1994.

Baladhuri, *Futuh al-Buldan*, Beirut, 1991.

Bayhaqi, Abu Bakr, *Ahkam al-Quran*, Beirut, vol. II, 1975.

———, *Al-Sunan al-Kubra*, Hyderabad, AH 1354.

Baydhavi, *Usul al-Baydhavi*, Istanbul, vol. IV, 1308.

Babarti, *Al-'Anayah*, Cairo, AH 1410.

Bukhari, M. bin Ism'ail, *Al-Jami al-Sahih*, Leiden: E.J. Brill, 1908.

Farsi, Abu 'Ali, *Jawahir al-Usul*, Medina, 1969.

Fasi, M. bin al-Hassan, *Al-Fikr al-Sami*, Medina, 1977.

Gangohi, H., *Zufr al-Muhasilin*, Delhi, 1996.

Ghazali, Abu Hamid, *ahya al-Ulum al-Din*, Beirut, 4 vols., 1990.

Haji Khalifah, *Kashf al-Dhunun*, Istanbul, 1941.

Haythami, Ibn Hajr, *Al-Fatawa al-Kubra*, Cairo, vol. IV, 1938.

Ibn Hauqal, *Surat al-Arz*, Iran, AH 1345.

Ibn Nadeem, *Al-Fihrist*, Cairo, AH 1360.

Ibn al-Athir, *Al-Kamil-fi-Tarikh*, Lebanon, 1987.

Isfahani, F., *Mehmannama Bukhara*, Tehran, 1962.

Ibn Hazam, M., *Mujam al-Fiqh*, Damascus, 1966.

Ibn al-Jauzi, *A'lam al-Muaqi'in*, Lebanon, 1979.

Ibn Khuldun, *Muqadimah*, New York, 1958.

Ibn Khalikan, *Wafiyat al-A'yan*, Beirut, vol. VIII, 1977.

Ibn Qatlubigah, *Taj al-Tarajim*, Baghdad, 1962.

Ibn Rushd, *Bidayat al-Mujtahid*, Beirut, vol. II, 1986.

Jurjani, al-Syed, *Al-Tarifat*, Cairo, 1938.

Kahalah, 'Umar Raza, *Mujam al-Musanifin*, Damascus, 1957.

Kasani, 'Alaudin, *Badaya al-Sunaya*, Beirut, vol. VII, 1982.

Khizr, M. Bik, *Tarakh al-Umam*, Egypt, 1938.

Khawarizmi, M., *Mafatih al'-Ulum*, Leaden: E.J. Brill, 1968.

Karkhi, *'Ubaydullah, Risalah al-Usul*, n.d.

Lakhnavi, Abul Hai, *Al-fawaid al-Bahiya*, Banaras, 1968.

Maqdisi, Al, *Ahsan al-Taqasim fi-marifat al-Aqalim*, Leiden, 1906.

Maraghi, 'Abdullah, *Al-Fatah al-Mubin*, Beirut, 1974.

Marghinani, 'Ali, *Al-Hidayah*, Delhi, vol. II, 1925.

Marwadi, 'Ali, *Ahkam al-Sultaniyah*, Cairo, 1960.

Muslim, Al-Qusheri, *Al-Sahih*, Cairo, vol V., 1955.

Narshakhi, *Tarikh-i-Bukhra*, Tashqand, 1897.

Nasafi, Najmudin, *Talbat al-Talba*, Baghdad, 1900.

Neshapuri, Asad, *Al-Furuq al-Karabisi*, Kuwait, AH 1401.

Nasfi, Abu Barkat, *Kashf al-Asrar*, Cairo, 1898.

Qarshi, 'Abdul Qadir, *Al-Jawahir al-Muziyah*, Hyderabad, AH 1332.

Qarafi, Shahbudin, *Mukhtasar Tanqih*, Damascus, n.d.

Qarzavi, Yusuf, *Fiqh al-Zakat*, Egypt, 1999.

Razi, Fakhrudin, *Majmu al-Rasail*, Cairo, 1973.

———, *Manazirat fi Bilad-i-Mawar al-Nahr*, Beirut, 1966.

Shashi, Ahmad, *Usul al-Shashi*, Beirut, 1982.

Sarakhsi, Muhammad, *Al-Usul*, Cairo, 1973.

———, *Al-Mabsut*, Karachi, 1987.

Shahristani, A. Karim, *Al-Milal Wa al-Nihl*, Cairo, 1968.

Sayyuti, Jalaludin, *Tarikh al-Khulafa*, Deoband, 1989.

Shatibi, Abu Ishaq, *Al-Muwafaqat*, Cairo, 1970.

Shirazi, Abu Ishaq, *Al-Luma-fi al-Usul*, Cairo, 1908

Sidiq Hassan, *Husul al-Ma'mul*, Istanbul, 1878.

Subki, Tajudin, *Tabaqat al-Kubra*, Cairo, 1906.

Taftazani, Sa'ad Din, *Hashiyah al-Sharah*, Cairo, vol. II, 1973.

Tabari, Ibn Jarir, *Tarikh al-Tabari*, Deoband, 1999.

Thanavi, Muhammad, *Kashf al-Istilahat al-Funun*, Calcutta, 1862.

Tabakh, Al-Raghib, *Tarikh Afkar al-Ulum al-Islami*, Delhi, 1982.

Tamimi, A. Qadir, *Al-Tabaqat al-Saniyahfi-Tarajim al-Hanafiyah*, Cairo, 1970.

Umar, Al-Nasafi, *Al-Qand fi-Zikr-i-Ulama-i-Samarqand*, Saudi Arabia, 1987.

Wansharsi, Ahmad, *Al-Miy'ar-al-fatawa*, Beirut, 1981.

Waliallah, Shah, *Al-Insaf fi-Bayan-i-Sabab-i-Ikhtilaf*, Delhi, 1953

Yaqut, Hamavi, *Mujam al-Buldan*, Cairo, 1906.

Yezdi, *Zafar Namah*, Calcutta, 1888.

Zarqashi, *Al-Sharah*, Cairo, n.d.

Zarqani, *Muwahib al-Luduniyah*, Cairo, AH 1291.

Zarkali, *Al-A'lam*, Beirut, 1953.

Secondary Sources

Abdul Rahim, *The Principles of Islamic Jurisprudence*, Delhi, 1994.

Aghnides, Nicholas, *Muhammadan Theories of Finance*, New York, 1916.

Arnold, T.W., *The Preaching of Islam*, Delhi, 1995.

Ahmad, M., *The Urgency of Ijtihad*, New Delhi, 1992.

Amin, S.H., *Islamic Law and Its Implications for Modern World*, Royston, U.K., 1989.

Amini, Taqi, *Fiqh-i-Islami ka Tarkhi Pas Manzar*, Delhi, 1973.

Azami, M.M., *On Schacht's Origins of Muhammadan Jurisprudence*, New York, 1985.

Arbery, A.J., *The Legacy of Persia*, London, 1968.

Athar, Hussain, *The Glorious Caliphate*, Lucknow, 1980.

Bergzmark, *Economic Geography of Asia*, New York, 1937.

Bosworth, *The Islamic Surveys*, Edinburgh, 1967.

Brockelman, N.C., *History of Islamic Peoples*, Leiden, 1969.

Brown, *Literary History of Persia*, Leiden, 1921.

Bukhari, H.N., *Muzakira Ahbab*, Delhi, 1969.

Coulson, N.J, *A History of Islamic Law*, Edinburgh, 1990.

———, *Conflicts and Tensions in Islamic Jurisprudence*, Chicago, 1969.

Denis, Sinor, *The Cambridge History of Early Inner Asia*, Cambridge, 1990.

Donaldson, D.M., *Studies in Muslim Ethics*, London, 1953.

Fayzee, A.A., *Outlines of Muhammadan Law*, London, 1960.

Gibb, H.A.R., *Muhammadanism*, London, 1963.

———, *The Arab Conquests in Central Asia*, New York, 1970.

Goldziher, *Introduction to Islamic Theology and Law*, Princeton, 1981.

Haider, Dughlat, *Tarikh-i-Rashidi*, Patna, 1973.

Hallaq, W.B., *A History of Islamic Legal Theories*, Cambridge, 1997.

Hitti, P.K., *History of the Arabs*, London, 1940.

Hussain, Showkat, "A Critical Study of Al-Farghani's Treatment of the Sources" in *al-Hidayah*, Sri Nagar, 2004.

Juynboll, G.H.A., *Studies on the First Century of Islamic Society*, Cambridge, 1982.

Juwaini, *Tarikh-i-Jehan Kusha*, Leiden, 1911.

Kunitiz, J., *Dawn over Samarkand*, Calcutta, 1943.

Kamali, M.H., *Principles of Islamic Jurisprudence*, Cambridge, 1991.

Krader, Lawrence, *Peoples of Central Asia*, The Hague, 1966.

Khudri, M. and H.J. Libesny, *Law in the Middle East: Origin and Development of Islamic Law*, Washington, 1955.

Khudri, M., *Tarikh-i-Tashrih al-Islami*, Cairo, 1967.

Levy, Rubin, *Social Structural of Islam*, Cambridge, 1962.

Le-strange, D., *The Lands of Eastern Caliphate*, Cambridge, 1930.

Levis, Bernard, *Islam from the Prophet Muhammad to the Capture of Constantinople*, USA, 1974.

Lukkegard, J.N., *Islamic Taxation in the Classic Period*, Copenhagen, 1950.

Lutfi, H., *Masters of the Wisdom of Central Asia*, Cambridge, 1962.

Linant, D.B., *The Formal Sources of Islamic Law*, New York, 1975.

Margoloith, D.S., *The Early Development of Muhammadanism*, London, 1919.

Mansura, Haider, *Central Asia in the Sixteenth Century*, Delhi, 2002.

Macdonald, B.D., *Development of Theology Jurisprudence and Constitutional Theory*, Cambridge, 1903.

Masud al-Hassan, *History of Islam*, Delhi, vol. II, 2006.

Nasr, S. Hussain and Oliver Leaman, *History of Islamic Philosophy*, Britain, 1996.

Oman, C.W.C., *The Art of War in Middle Ages*, New York, 1960.

Parker, E.H., *A Thousand Years of the Tatars*, London, 1885.

Parry, V.J. and M.E. Yaap, *War Technology and Society in The Middle East*, London, 1975.

Qureshi, T.A., *Methodologies of Social Change and Islamic Law*, Pakistan, 1987.

Rasheed, Ahmad, *The Resurgence of Central Asia*, London, 1996.

Riaz, A. Islam, *Indo-Persian Relations*, Tehran, 1970.

Richards, D.S., *Islam and the Trade of Asia*, Oxford, 1970.

Richmers, W., *The Duab of Turkistan*, Cambridge, 1913.

Ronald, S. and R. Susan, *Islam and Central Asia*, Washington, 2006.

Rypka, J., *History of Persian Literature*, Tehran, 1968.

Sarwar, G., *History of Shah Ismail Safavi*, Aligarh, 1939.

Saulat, S., *Milat-i-Islamia Ki Mukhtasar Tarikh*, Delhi, vol. IV, 1994.

Schacht, Joseph, *The Origins of Muhammadan Jurisprudence*, Oxford, 1950.

———, *An Introduction to Islamic Law*, Oxford, 1964.

Schuylaer, E., *Turkish Notes of Journey in Russian Turkistan Khokand Bukhara and Khiva*, London, 1876.

Shabir, A., *Islam Mein 'Ilm Wa Hikmat Ka Agaz*, Azamgarah, n.d.

Smith, W.C., *On Understanding Islam*, The Hague, Mouton Publishers 1981, p. 344.

Shahpuri, Abad, *Rus Mein Musalman Qumain*, Delhi, 1987.

Shaban, M.A., *The Abbassid Revolution*, Cambridge, 1970.

Shalbi, A., *History of Muslim Education*, Beirut, 1954.

Sharief, M.M., *A History of Muslim Philosophy*, Delhi, 2 vols., 1989.

Suhraev, *Bukhara*, Moscow, 1966.

Shemesh, A.B., *Taxation in Islam*, Leiden, 1967.

Tibbi, Bassam, *Islam and Cultural Accommodation of Social Change*, Oxford, 1991.

Tahir, Muhammad, *Islamic Institutions*, New Delhi, 1998.

Watt, W.M., *Islam and the Integration of Society*, London, 1970.

———, *The Formative Period of Islamic Thought*, Edinburgh, 1973.

Wolf, J., *Narrative of a Mission to Bukhara*, New York, 1845.

Waliullah, M., *Muhammadan Jurisprudence and Quranic Law of Crimes*, Delhi, 1986.

Zia-al-Huq, *Revelation and Revolution in Islam*, Delhi, 1982.

Zubaida, S. Islam, *The People and the State*, London, 1989.

Encyclopaedias

Arab Islamic Bibliography, Grimwood Jones, Harvester Press, London.

A Basic Bibliography of Islam, Cairo, 1952.

Bibliography of Works Dealing with Islam

The Cambridge History of Iran, T.P. Huges, London.

The Cambridge History of Islam, ed. P.M. Holt, London.

The Concise Encyclopaedia of Islam, Glasse, 1989.

Dairat al-Ma'arif, Danishgah-i-Punjab, Lahore, 1997.

Dairat al-Ma'arif, Syed Sabahudin, Delhi, 1984.

Encyclopaedia of Islam, Leiden: E.J. Brill, 1953.

Encyclopaedia of Islamic Law, Laleh Bakhtiyar, Chicago, 1995.

Encyclopaedia of Religion and Ethics, Oxford.

Oxford Encyclopaedia of Modern Islamic World, Oxford, 1995.

Journals and Periodicals

American Journal of Comparative Law, vol. 50, 2002.

Central Asian Journal, 2001.

Central Asiatic Journal, vol. I, 1955.

Hamdard Islamicus, Pakistan, vol. XXIII (1), January-March 2000.

Harvard Journal of Asiatic Studies, vol. LX.

Indiana International and Comparative Review, vol. XVII.

International Journal of Islamic & Arabic Studies, 1985.

International Journal of Middle East Studies, vol. XXXII, 2000.
Islamic Culture, 1960.
Islamic Law & Society, vol. I-VII, 1994–2000.
Islamic Quarterly, 1967.
The Journal of Asian Studies, vol. 63, 2004.
Journal of Islamic Studies, 1992.
Journal of Near Eastern Studies, vol. LX, 2002.
Journal of Religious Ethics, 1983.
Journal of Royal Asiatic Society, vol. XVI, 1910.
Journal of School of Advanced Study in Social Sciences, 1982.
Journal of the American Oriental Society, vol. 122, 2002.
Journal of the Arabic Oriental Society, 1986.
Law-Liberty Journal, vol. 93(2), 2001.
Middle East Studies, 1978.
New York University Journal of International Law & Politics, 1979.

Index